Becca & John,

Happy readin',
y'all!

T— Dillard

THE WORD AROUND TOWN
ON TAVIN'S BOOK,
TEAM BURGER SHED

"There ain't enough pictures."

— Delma Spencer, momma and
attempted firework thief

"This book goes great with any donut."

— Cheryl Grubbs, owner of Donut Goals

"I'm happy that my burgers feed the team's bellies and my shirts cover those bellies up."

— Bud, owner of the Burger Shed

"You take a phone book, some plywood, and the *Team Burger Shed* book, you got a pretty decent remote control car ramp."

— Bret Dillard, Tavin's brother

"This book is big enough to set a small bowl of deer chili and your car keys on."

— Donnie Wayne Chambliss, owner of the
repair shed by the lake

"We always like more reading material for the gals."

— Gracie Dilroy, owner of
Early Bird Gets the Perm

"*Team Burger Shed* is my backup door stop. Cinder block is still my first choice."

— Memaw

TEAM BURGER SHED

THE BOOK

TAVIN DILLARD

TEAM BURGER SHED

Copyright © 2024 by Joel Berry

ISBN: 978-1-951305-70-3
Also available in eBook and Audiobook.

Connect with Tavin Dillard at www.SweetTeaFilms.com.

Cover photo: Mason Berry
Photo assistant: Dylan Berry

Printed in the United States of America.

BEST MEDICINE BOOKS
A STORY WARREN IMPRINT
www.StoryWarren.com

CONTENTS

Map 7

Foreword 9

Editor's note 11

1. Preseason 13
2. Skins 27
3. Turtle Party 43
4. Shirts 59
5. Dinner Rolls 71
6. S'mores 83
7. Crows 99
8. Jawbreaker 111
9. Ice Cream 121

10. Jalapeño. 131

11. Kitty Cat 141

12. Donuts 149

13. One Innin'. 159

14. Tires 171

15. Team Party 181

About Tavin Dillard 186

About Joel Berry 187

Get More from Tavin. 188

A MAP OF TAVIN'S TOWN

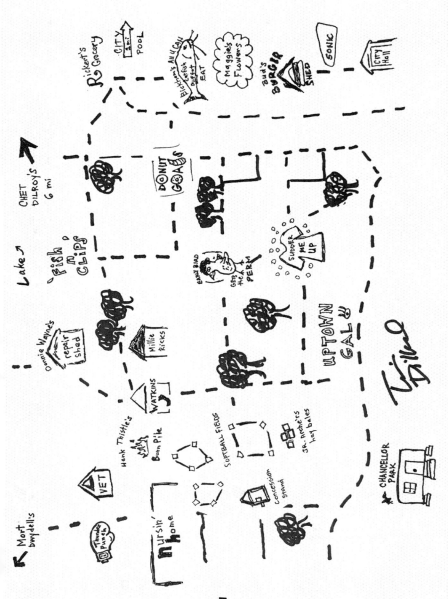

FOREWORD

Some people say, "I can't recommend this enough!" But some people add a period. "I can't recommend this. Enough!" That's how close we are to saying the exact opposite. One teensy little punctuation mark.

I'm S. D. Smith, author of *Mooses with Bazookas: And Other Stories Children Should Never Read*. So, you should probably take me very seriously as a very serious author of very serious books that are serious.

I grew up in the hills and hollers of West Virginia. Well, not all of them, but you get the idea. My dad said we lived so far back in the woods that no one lived behind us. I thought he was serious for the longest time.

TEAM BURGER SHED

I was in California for some reason once, and there was a guy from Arkansas there who said he was glad I was there so no one would make fun of him. He saw me as a kind of protective hillbilly shield. True story. We became friends because one thing is, people from Arkansas and West Virginia don't usually get too big for their britches. There's another feller from Arkansas who I also met in California. (If you take nothing else away from this, Sherlock, you have learned that the best place to meet Arkansans is in California.) Anyway, this new Arkansan was named Tavin Dillard. Still is named Tavin Dillard. He's kept it this entire time. Matter of fact, you're holding his book right now.

Despite the abuse some Arkansans have heaped upon me and my people, I love Tavin Dillard. He is a legend in my home and in his own watermelon-helmet-covered mind. What you are about to read will do you real good, especially if you are eager for chuckles. Chuckles are hard to come by these days, with inflation what it is. Do yourself a favor and enjoy this literary feast. Is it more sno-cones, hot fries, and donuts than a fancy French dinner? Yes. Thank goodness.

I cannot recommend this enough!

S. D. Smith

Editor's Note

Welcome to the world of Tavin Dillard. There's no easy way to explain the wonderful world you're entering. There's a rhythm to how Tavin tells a story. Rather than me trying to describe it, your best bet is to meet Tavin. Visit this web address: StoryWarren.com/Tavin or scan the QR code below to watch a video of Tavin introducing this book.

You're going to have so much fun!
Editor

PRESEASON

S ome things are easy for folks. Like rampin' a bike over a creek is easy for Rusty Tidwell. Then sometimes easy things are hard. Like it's easy for me to drink a glass of milk, but Mort Dwydell can't have no dairy.

We all got our things, and when it's happenin' to you it's a big deal. That's just how it is.

So, what if I seen a gal, who ain't lived in my town in years, deliverin' produce to the Burger Shed?

Just go say hi to her, Tavin, you might say.

Next time I see her, I'm liable to. It ain't that it's hard; it just ain't easy. But let's not get ahead of ourselves.

I have gotten pretty good at lawn mowin'. I'll tell ya right now that there is a whole lot that comes along with this job. A whole lot.

Like what, Tavin?

I'm glad ya asked. Firstlys, people want to talk. They want to chat about the weather, produce, their grandbabies, you name it. And you know what I do? I listen.

And folks is always cookin'. You know about that? They want to share food with anybody that stops by and, as a lawnmowin' man, I'm always stoppin' by.

One day recently I mowed Imogene and Raymond Watkins's lawn. If you know anything about Raymond and Imogene's house, you know they got a nice porch swing to the left of the front door. And it's about six or seven steps to get onto that porch.

So, I'm basically done with their lawn. It's a good size lawn, and their backyard ain't small neither. And here I am done with the work. Imogene steps out on the front porch and asks me that very same thing.

"You all done?"

"Sure am, Imogene!" I hollered back.

Raymond was messin' with the flower bed in front of their porch while Imogene waved me over.

Now, I didn't know if she had some cookies, bread,

casserole, or some old sweat breeches she wanted to pass off to me, but I figure it was somethin'. Then she told me, "I got some ice water for ya."

I'm used to Imogene doin' that, so I don't usually bring no water to drink when I mow her lawn.

And then Raymond chimed in, "She makes a real good glass of ice water."

"Don't I know it," I hollered back to Raymond.

I leave my mower there on the front lawn, along with my bike, and head up them steps into their house, followin' Imogene.

Once you step into Imogene and Raymond's house, there's a sittin' room on the left. That's where you sit. To the right is a livin' room. That's where you live.

"Take a seat there, Tavin. I'll be back directly," Imogene calls as she shuffles into the kitchen.

So, I take a seat in the sittin' room. There's a couple small couches there that face each other. Between them is a glass coffee table that's got that plastic fruit in a bowl. It ain't real food. Don't try and eat it. Lesson learned. But if you do, just turn the fruit over.

Before too long Imogene makes her way back to the sittin' room with a big ol' glass of ice water. Like a heavy glass. She don't believe in paper or plastic throwaway picnic cups. Even at a picnic, she says, "Them drinks sure would taste better in a real glass."

The glass is heavy. Imogene don't care. She even told me.

"You know, Raymond and I go through a gallon of milk a week. We got strong bones."

"Is that so, Imogene?"

"Oh, yeah. I fell off the back porch last week and didn't get hurt at all."

"Really?" I asked her as she got closer with that big ol' glass of ice water.

"That's right, but I can't say the same for the azalea bush."

And Imogene just snickers about that. She finally hands me the glass of water. Raymond was right. She makes a good glass of ice water.

Now in her other hand she was holdin' somethin'. I really wasn't sure what, mostly because I was focused on the water. Then she extended her hand out to me. And you know how when somebody offers you somethin' you just instinctively reach your hand out to take what they're offerin'? Well, that's what I did.

I set down the water and just reach out to take whatever Imogene is givin' me. And she's so happy to share.

Reason how come I know is because she's smilin' ear to ear.

Now, I'm lookin' in my hand and what I see is a very black nanner.[1]

I'm lookin' at that thing, and I start to wonder if she's puttin' a dead crow in my hand. But then I was thinkin' that I don't see no beak on that thing. And I figure Imogene wouldn't have taken the time to de-beak a crow.

It's all happenin' so fast, and this is where my mind is goin'. So, now I got a pitch-black nanner in my hand, and I don't want to be rude, but I don't know what to do. It's way overripe. I mean a midnight, pitch-black, lights out, not-wakin'-up nanner.

It ain't just that I'm holdin' that nasty thing in my hand like a baby hairless cat, but I'm also gettin' the sense that Imogene wants me to do somethin' with that nanner right now. Thing about it is, I don't want to do anything with it except throw it away.

At this point, I start hatchin' my own plan, as they say. Like a crow egg from a healthy crow. I'm thinkin' that maybe I can get out of here with this black nanner and make it up to Hank Thistle's yard.

Hank's got a burn pile goin' year-round. I figure

---

1. *Editor's note: A very black banana.*

if I can get up there, that I'll throw this very black, get-under-the-covers-close-your-eyes nanner right on that burn pile. Sounds like a good idea to me.

One thing I ain't mentioned yet is that this nanner is pretty tender. You know how black it is, but it's also tender like Myron Curtis's guts. I notice my thumb has kinda gone into this thing. Now I smell it.

So I try and stand up to leave. This is the time to get out of here.

I start to thank Imogene for the gifts. As I stand, *she* stands and reaches out and just taps both my shoulders like the wings of a crow.

"Have a seat."

She is ready to watch me eat this thing. Now I know that there is only one way out of this house, and it's through this very black nanner. So, I sit back down, and Imogene does too. She's got her hands under her chin kinda clappin'. You know how a momma is at a school play watchin' her kid be Tree Number Three and she's so proud? That's how Imogene looked. It's like it did her heart good to see me eat healthy.

Here I am sittin' with this black nanner while Imogene perches across from me. I don't dry heave in front of her. But I do try to peel this thing. It is way overripe. Blindfold yourself, sit in a closet, close the door, and you can't see that nanner. Pitch-black.

I'm like a toddler with a sloppy joe. Truth be told, I'm like an adult with a sloppy joe. I figure I gotta start gettin' this down instead of spreadin' it everywhere. So, I start eatin' this nanner out of the palm of my hand.

Only thing is, I can't tell what's nanner and what's peel. I don't want to eat the peel. And Imogene is across from me just so happy. Like this is all goin' exactly how she hoped.

I don't even know what to do at this point. I ain't never ate a hairless cat before, but I got to think that I'm gettin' close to what it would be like. I was lickin' that thing—in between my fingers, now it's on the back of my hand, everywhere. I look over and lock eyes with Imogene. All the while my hands are covered, draped, marinated in very black nanner. I mean very black.

She looks like she just won free tickets to the County Fair Barbecue Picnic Pavilion. And they have them free sodas there too.

She is startin' to notice the mess and asks if I need a napkin. I tell her I do, and she hurries out, returnin' with a tiny tissue. And I'm pretty sure it was one ply.

Well, she drops that in my hand, and it basically disappears. Now I don't know what's nanner, what's peel, and what's tissue. I know I can't eat it all because then I'd be eatin' peel and tissue for sure. So, I decide to make a move.

I stand up and try to maneuver out of that sittin' room. And she lets me go! So, now I'm headin' toward the front door, both hands covered in very black nanner, and I got no idea how I'm gonna get that doorknob.

Imogene shuffles by and grabs the doorknob for me. Thank you, Imogene.

Well, I get on that front porch and look down at them hands of mine. I close my hands, and it sounds like a bike tire goin' through mud—nanner squishin' everywhere.

I head down them porch steps, and now I'm lookin' down at my shirt. I gotta get this nanner off my hands. I'm gonna have to go home and change my shirt in the middle of the day if I do that. Then I look out over Imogene and Raymond Watkin's freshly mowed lawn.

I step onto that lawn, drop to my knees, and start wipin' my hands all over it. Then from behind me I hear, "You sure like your job, don't ya?"

I peek back over my shoulder, and there is Raymond on that porch swing thinkin' I'm down there on my hands and knees just enjoyin' that fresh-cut lawn I mowed.

"I sure do. I really do, Raymond," I call back as I rise to my feet.

Then I do one of them straight-legged walk-runs when you want to get out of somewhere, but you don't want them to think you're sprintin' away. I tie my lawnmower to my bike seat with my rope, and I'm outta there!

It wasn't too long before I rode past Hank Thistle's burn pile. And today it smelled a little like leaves and a whole lot like regret.

I end up goin' back to the trailer to clean up anyway. I figure I'd rather smell like Pert Plus than black nanner. So, I did that and then went to fetch some lunch.

As I walk into the Burger Shed, there in a booth is Mort Dwydell and Myron Curtis. Myron's back is to the door, but I know what he looks like. Mort is facin' the door.

Bud saw me walk in, and they start gettin' my number three combo meal started. That's a bacon double cheeseburger, Dr Pepper, and curly fries. Myron turns around in that booth, and his eyes is all wide like a possum in a trash can.

He waves me over to the booth, and I can tell somethin' is goin' on. They are steady thinkin' hard like they're workin' on remedial fractions. So, I make it over to their booth, and Myron just says, "Tavin, it's softball season."

"Okay, Myron."

Let me give you some background on town softball in case this ain't somethin' that happens in your neck of the woods. First of all, it's always goin' like a mighty river. It's just always there. Softball don't stop. No big deal, right?

Well, as Myron extends the invite on this afternoon in the Burger Shed, somethin' grabs me. I even think I hear a little bit of "Chariots of Fire." I get lost in the moment for a bit.

For some reason I see this picture of the adult softball season for what it really is: stories told, legends bein' born, friendships strengthened, a mild resemblance to exercise, and free sno-cones on Thursday nights if your team wins.

"Hey, Tavin! You there?"

Mort Dwydell bolts to attention and is now standin' next to me. He is lookin' like he's ready to jump to action.

"I thought you had a stroke, Tavin. I was ready to

do the Heimlich on you," Mort exclaimed.

I was like, "I don't think that's how it works, Mort."

They asked me if I was in. I told them I sure was. That's when Myron said, "Great. That'll be twenty dollars."

So I hand over some of that hard-earned cash that I had to endure a black nanner for. I figure since I was in now I should be able to ask questions. So, I do.

"What's our team name?"

"We ain't got a name yet, Tavin."

"You got a sponsor?"

"No, we ain't got no sponsor."

"Well, that usually helps you with the team name."

Myron nods.

I think, well if they ain't got a name and they ain't got a sponsor, the next logical question is, "What *can* you tell me, Myron?"

He said, "We need two more guys for a full roster."

So, quick math tells me they needed three when I walked into the Burger Shed, and now they only need two more players.

Myron proceeds to assure me that once they get the rest of the roster filled out, he'd order the uniforms, and they would be at the fields the first game next week. Myron and Mort got softball deadlines steady comin' at them, so they gonna be busy this week.

Now, about this time Mary Beth Tucker enters the Burger Shed. She's my best friend Russell Tucker's little sister. She got married young, right out of high school, and that didn't work out. She's a good ol' girl. She went to school for horses. Her and Russell come from kinda husky stock. She's a smart girl, knows a lot about animals, and works down at the veterinary.

Myron seen her walk in there, and he can't take his eyes off her. He's wide-eyed. No poker face or nothin'.

Mort says, "Why don't you take a picture; it'll last longer."

And Myron's like, "I ain't no weirdo!"

I said, "Easy, fellas. We're all friends here."

Then I just call out to her, "Hey, Mary Beth!"

She says hey and makes her way over to our booth. I guess she is in there for some lunch. She don't seem to be in a big rush. She asks how we're doin'. Mort tells her that we are gettin' ready for softball season.

That's when Mary Beth says she'll be workin' the concession stand at the fields this season.

Well, Myron is still flustered, and like any good

friend I just say, "Hey, Mary Beth, Myron's got somethin' to say to you."

So, she turns and looks right at Myron. Truth be told, I thought he'd stay flustered, but he gets steady focused! Myron pulled it together in the moment.

He clears his throat and says, "Mary Beth, I got a new moped here recently for my birthday. It'd be my honor if I could pick you up tonight and take you to Bickham's All You Can Eat Catfish Buffet."

I'm shocked.

Mary Beth says, "Well, that sounds fun, Myron. How 'bout six thirty?"

He nods. Bud calls Mary Beth's order. Just a few moments ago Myron was bumblin' to pull our softball season together, and now he's got a date on his moped with Mary Beth Tucker to the catfish buffet.

Kinda made me think the next time I see that produce delivery gal I'll say hi. If Myron can do it, so can I.

And if Myron can talk to Mary Beth Tucker, he can have our roster full and uniforms ready at the fields for our first game next week.

I should probably start stretchin' my haunches now. I mean, I can play some ball, but I'm still a common man. So, I got to get ready. Preseason is upon us.

TEAM BURGER SHED

Next week we'll be together as a team with no name, stories will be born, legends will be made, and hopefully, I'll be gettin' a free sno-cone served up by Mary Beth Tucker at the concession stand.

SKINS

Last week Myron Curtis asked Mary Beth Tucker out on their first date. We was all surprised at how fast that happened. Myron ain't what you would call a Casanova, and Mary Beth has standards. Well, long story longer, they had their first date.

I don't understand why Myron's version of puttin' his best foot forward is pickin' Mary Beth up on his moped. Myron carries some girth, and Mary Beth is big boned. You already know she's Russell Tucker's little sister. Russell's over six foot tall. So, you take that girth of Myron and that stock of Mary Beth, and you put that on a standard moped, you steady testin' the weight limit and strength of that vehicle's frame.

I mean, it's doin' all it can to do what it's supposed to do. That thing tops out at thirty-two miles an hour, but if Myron gunned that thing the best it was gonna do with both of them on there is a solid twenty-six miles an hour. And that's how that goes.

How'd their date go? Oh, buddy, it went.

Myron took her to Bickham's All You Can Eat Catfish Buffet. Tuesday nights is coupon night and nanner puddin'. Made with ripe nanners best I can tell. The prices are good, and it's a popular night in town, no doubt about it.

Myron parks that moped in the parkin' lot. Bickham's ain't got moped parkin'. He just has to slide into a standard parkin' spot. I give Mary Beth credit for lettin' him take her there on that thing.

Was it a good start? Well, Myron didn't lay that thing down on the way there. Road rash ain't no way to start a first date. So far, so good.

If you ain't never been to Bickham's, it's probably good for you to know that it's been Bickham's for a number of years. Decades. Now, it wadn't built to be a catfish buffet in the beginnin'. It was a bank and then a sportin' goods store, and this is the third thing that it has been.

Folks love it. They show it with their pocketbook.

You know about that? When folks spend their money on somethin', they are sendin' a message. And I ain't a pocketbook-ologist, but I figure what it means is that folks like the food at Bickham's All You Can Eat Catfish Buffet.

And, of course, the headliner has to deliver. The catfish is good. Real good. How's the service? Not terrible. Thing about it is, when the product is real good, folks can forgive just decent service. Reason how come is that we just figure, "Oh, they probably busy makin' this food taste so good, that's why they ain't refilled this ketchup bottle on the table yet," like attaway.

Travis Darden has been runnin' it for about fifteen years now. His uncle Arlo started it originally.

They got your standard situation with the ice cream machine at Bickham's. When it's workin', there ain't no better way to cap off a great meal. But when it's broke, it can be real disappointin' if you been thinkin' about it all meal long. The buffet has fried okra, green beans, hushpuppies, macaroni and cheese, corn, turnip greens, and, of course, catfish. Lots and lots of catfish.

Myron and Mary Beth got healthy appetites. I guess this is the one time when we use the word *healthy* and it sounds unhealthy. Once you tell somebody that a person has a healthy appetite, we just kinda imagine them with a plate full of chicken wings and Snickers bars and they drinkin' Dr Pepper straight from the two-liter. Healthy.

All I'm sayin' is that Myron and Mary Beth ain't got issues with gettin' their money's worth at any dinin' establishment. And their first date was no different.

They both pile their plates high with fried okra, hushpuppies, catfish fillets. Now, if you know anything about *fillets*—that's probably Latin or somethin' for "We took the bone out." There ain't supposed to be no bone in a catfish fillet, and you know there's some tiny bones in the ol' catfish.

Well, Mary Beth got to chokin'. I mean, she has tored through a plate of okra and green beans and I guess has saved the best for last. She inhaled some catfish, her air pipe clogs, and she is steady chokin'. I don't guess there had been much conversation in the date up until this point anyway. It has mostly been puttin' a hurtin' on that buffet and kinda starin' at each other.

Well, turns out Mary Beth is gonna need some help. So, Myron shuffles around behind her and tries to hinelack[2] her. I don't guess he's never been trained, but I think he just seen it in a movie or somethin'. So, the short story is, he don't know what he's doin'. He start tryin' to hinelack her, and it ain't workin'. At all.

Mary Beth is gettin' mad. She's elbowin' him— just a steady stream of elbows to the rib cage. She can't talk, and she needs him to cut it out. He ain't helpin'.

She pushes back from the table, stands up, and leans herself over a sturdy chair, and she hinelacks herself. That bone just shot out like Old Faithful. Archin' through the air and landin' on the other side of the table.

Myron is mad. He's embarrassed that he couldn't hinelack her, and he's also mad because there is supposed to be no bone in that catfish. So, he's off to the kitchen. Travis Darden is in there, and Myron swings open them doors like he's an outlaw in a saloon.

He tells Travis somethin' like I'm madder than a wet peacock in a henhouse. Nobody really knows what he means, but he says it in a way that folks could figure he was pretty mad. Myron tells him he's gotta make this right! Travis agrees and gives them free coupons to next week's buffet.

Well, that worked out for them. Mary Beth ends

---

2. *Editor's note: Heimlich, as in Heimlich maneuver.*

up finishin' her meal. She seems okay, but I think to get ready for next week Myron needs to take a first aid class or CPR. Wouldn't hurt.

Who cares, right? What about the first softball game, Tavin? That's probably what you are askin'.

Well, it ain't no secret Myron was a lil' preoccupied this week with his date. And him and Mary Beth seem to be likin' each other. So, I'll mark his loose first day up to that.

Why do I say loose?

Firstlys, what time is our first game? Nobody knows. Myron has the schedule, but he ain't told folks. So, fellas show up after work and supper, and thankfully we don't have no early five p.m. game. We are the seven p.m. game. We get to the field and I ask Myron about the uniforms. Oh, buddy. He stares at me like I just spoke to him in algebra.

Mort chimes in, "Myron! Where are the uniforms?"

Myron shakes his head. "I completely forgot to pick them up."

"Should we go get them?"

Myron shakes his head. "Let's just use the shirts we got for tonight." Well, Rusty Tidwell has on a work shirt. I don't have on a shirt because I had just pulled it off to wipe off all the sweat after mowin' lawns, and, you can imagine, nobody is real happy to start off the season with no uniforms. So, I suggest we do skins.

Myron said, "Oh, Tavin. I don't know. Mary Beth is workin' the concession stand tonight, and I don't wanna be runnin' around shirtless. That's embarrassin'."

"I don't guess none of us do, Myron, but we ain't got much of a choice."

JT Whitlow chimes in and says Myron has his head in the clouds. And Rusty asks him if the uniforms will be ready next game. Myron says he'd have 'em.

So, we ain't too far from game time, and we gotta figure out our lineup. Then we just kinda put it outta our minds that we are all chest-naked. Tall order. Or a wide order in some of our cases.

Fellas are shakin' their heads at Myron as he tries to scribble down a battin' order on an index card.

Weather was nice. We played Team Sonic. They're already intimidatin' just by showin' up in uniforms. But we have to push on in spite of the circumstances.

I feel like I should back up and state the question everybody is askin'. Is Myron Curtis in charge of this team? Is he the coach? Because it seems like, despite all odds, Myron is the catalyst in gettin' this team together.

Well, you ever heard of the sayin' "He knows just enough about that to get into trouble?" Well, Mort and Myron know enough about softball season to get the ball rollin'. Mort had seen the sign-ups, and the city planner Tommy Standridge had told Mort he needed to get a team together. And that's really all it takes.

It's like if you walk into a group of elementary school kids and say y'all should run laps and, who knows, y'all may be in the Olympics one day. Well, there's a lot that needs to happen between them laps around the playground and the Olympics, but they just doin' what they know—runnin' in circles.

So, yeah, Mort and Myron can get the sign-ups together and collect money, but that ain't all it takes for what I would call a successful adult league softball season. Case in point, here we are standin' in front of the dugouts, game one, takin' off our shirts in front of the town because we ain't got uniforms.

Myron is flustered. He sees Mary Beth Tucker and lets out an audible *"eeho."* That ain't even a word. This is goin' sideways quick, and fellas are startin' to grumble.

I knew I could help some, but the best administrator and organizer in our group is Russell Tucker. You should see his garage. He's got that thing put together. I mean, he's got shelves for his shelves.

So I reach for the index card from Myron's hand as he has some sort of chest-naked meltdown. I feel like I hear the other team snickerin' across the way. The umpire has shown up now. It's Lonnie Gene Sturgis; he's the game warden and also has a hot dog food truck. We start feelin' like we are runnin' outta time.

And at this point it's easy to start gettin' down on yourself. Standin' there thinkin' about all the times in the winter when you said, "I should do a push-up. Boy, if I ever have to take my shirt off in public it sure would be nice to be kinda fit and toned. Hey, are those Strawberry Twinkies? I don't see them too often. And strawberries is fruit. Maybe I'll just have two."

I call to Russell Tucker, "Can you finish out this lineup card and take it to Lonnie Gene?" Then, I call to the team, "Fellas! Get in the dugout. They the home team."

I figured as much because they took the field. It's at this point when you want to remind yourself that this is small-town adult softball. It's supposed to be fun. It's supposed to be excitin'—but we were not close to excited.

While we are walkin' to the field, I see the produce delivery gal, her name is Cricket, headin' to a truck in the parkin' lot. Not sure what she was doin' at the fields, but I seen her. She didn't see me.

Brodie Childress pulls up in a two-toned '86 Buick Century blastin' some Def Leppard. He skids into a parkin' spot and hops out. Then he throws his keys at the concession stand wall like it was a valet who was supposed to catch 'em.

You may see stupid, but I saw our final teammate make it to the game. And now we are official.

"Brodie, get that shirt off and get over here!" I hope that's the last time that sentence ever exits my mouth. For sure it was the first.

Russell has me battin' leadoff, which ain't a bad call. I think the worst call for all of us is that we are horribly-to-mild-horribly out of shape. And there ain't nothin' you can do at this point but face the music. I mean, it's slow pitch softball. How embarrassin' can it be?

I step up to the plate, and Cody Mantel is pitchin' for Sonic. This guy is a stud. And he's mean. And he recently got outta jail. So, I step into the batter's box, and he brushes me back with an inside pitch. I hit the deck. I don't know what kinda field you think we play on, but it's gravelly. It's kinda that red infield dirt, and the city puts up them chalk lines around the edge, but I done messed up the batter's box thing, layin' there in the chalk like a crime scene outline.

Cody's laughin'.

"Somethin' funny, Cody?"

He nods. "You should see what I see."

"You better be glad you can see. I'm liable to drive this ball right at ya!"

Cody nods, pitches, and I watch a strike go right by. Out of emotion I want to swing as hard as I can, but I do the opposite. I just spectate. Then I have an idea.

Why don't I use my strengths? If I'm fast, why don't I just get down to first base? So, Cody pitches that next ball, and I drop the bat, sprint up the line, and dive headfirst, Pete Rose, chest-naked right into the bag. Safe!

I stand up, gravel skid up my chest. It's startin' to bleed.

Lonnie Gene calls out, "What are you doin', Tavin?"

I said, "I just stole first base, Lonnie Gene."

And he said, "You can't do that."

I said, "Did anybody tag me out?"

"No."

"Was that a legal slide?"

"No."

"No?"

Lonnie Gene said, "You can't slide without a uniform."

Hands on my hips, I turn and look at Myron Curtis in the dugout. I'm furious. How is he gonna take my one joy in adult league softball—the headfirst slide—and just disqualify it? Well, I feel like I've been pretty patient with Myron up until this point, but this is pushin' me to the limit.

Lonnie Gene calls out, "Come finish your at bat, Tavin." So, I make it back to the batter's box. Apparently, Cody had thrown another strike, so it was one-and-two, and I step back in.

Is this still the first at bat of the first game of the season? We gotta move this along.

So, I rear back and swing as hard as I can. Now I'm a lefty—that's how I got down the first base line so quick when I stole first. So, I make contact and spray that ball to left field. Well, if I had hit it harder, it woulda been left field. It went to the third baseman. One out.

The first innin' didn't get much better. JT Whitlow hits a dribbler to the first baseman, and then Mort Dwydell is up. If he gets on base, he's got Rusty Tidwell behind him, and that fella can rake.

Now, Mort is stout, little stubby legs, long torso. And he can hit dingers. But he's all or nothin'—he will hit a home run or get thrown out at first. He ain't a runner. He could hit what would be a double, maybe a triple, for most folks and get thrown out at first. He just likes the home run trot. No pressure at that point. And he swings for the fences every single time.

So, he climbs up there with two outs and do what he does. All the way to the wall. Long out. So, Rusty don't get a chance to bat in the first innin'.

Well, Team Sonic came ready to play. They score five runs in the first innin'. Everything seems to happen in slow motion. Rusty is our third baseman, and he just airmails a throw to Mort at first. Mort ain't real tall and his arms ain't long, so it's a bit of a mess.

We got through it. Some people have softball practice. Well, this first game is our first practice—put it to you that way.

Myron Curtis sees Mary Beth Tucker crane her neck outta the concession stand to see the action. Well, that's about the third innin', and that is when she realizes we are playin' shirts and skins. Myron locks eyes with her and kinda covers his chest, which I thought was gross.

"Come on, Myron. Get your head in the game."

"She seen me, Tavin."

"Well, that'll be a good test for the relationship. Now, do you want her to see you win or lose lookin' like this?"

Boy, that kinda inspired Myron, so he grabs a bat, strides chest-naked to the plate, his sweat shorts tied real snug, and he just starts hackin'.

I mean, he did have confidence, but that didn't change his skill level. He ended up reachin' first on a strikeout, wild pitch. That ball bounces into Team Sonic's dugout and rolls into a pile of softballs. It gets confusin', and the ump gives Myron first. We'll take it.

Battin' behind Myron Curtis is Brodie Childress, who lines one to the right field wall. He hits that thing so hard and so fast that it bounces back to their outfielder, and Myron only makes it to second base. Brodie is halfway to second when he realizes he's gotta go back. Then Russell Tucker hits a double, and Myron somehow motors in, and Brodie is on his heels.

And that, well, that's the highlights of game one, really. I mean, we score two runs, and it feels like we are movin' in the right direction. For a team to grind out two runs chest-naked with no practices kinda feels like a win.

Now, Team Sonic got hot in the fourth innin', and the only thing that slowed them down was the end of the game.

I'm losin' count, but I know while they push their tenth run across, Myron Curtis throws his shoe in their dugout. And he don't get it back until the end of the game. So, we got Myron on the infield—one cleat, one socked foot, chest-naked in sweat shorts and a ball cap with a glove on his hand. Quite a picture, but I tell ya at this point, I feel like Myron gets it. I have full confidence that he don't wanna be like this next week.

He said he'll pick up our uniforms, so I believe next week we'll have 'em. Will we be any better next week? Maybe not, but I don't think we left it all on the field tonight. Now, lookin' at Myron Curtis missin' a shoe, one might think otherwise, but it's the truth.

So, our nameless, shirtless team is now oh-and-one. Is it a bad start? I'd have to say so. Insalt[3] to

---

3. *Editor's note: Insult.*

41

injury, we went to get sno-cones after the game and had to watch Team Sonic get their free ones first.

Myron squeezed back into his T-shirt to get in line at the concession stand. Mary Beth Tucker is sayin' how proud she is of him. And he kinda smiles, holds up the line, and grosses out the team.

"How you like bein' skins, Myron?"

He shakes his head. "Hate it."

I smile. Ain't none of us really like that about tonight. I mean, I got road rash up my chest from that slide. It ain't gonna show up in the box score tomorrow, but I stoled first base. Everybody at the field tonight knows it too. Safe by a mile.

And game one is in the books.

Now, I'm thinkin' about how to see this gal Cricket again. I know she's deliverin' produce to the Burger Shed because I seen it with my own eyes. And I know my way to the Burger Shed.

I'm happy for Myron and Mary Beth. That's all good. But they ain't good for softball yet. The good news about sports is that the next game is a new start. And that game is just around the corner.

TURTLE PARTY

Once softball season starts, you can think everything else just stops. As fun as that sounds, it just ain't true. Life goes on. And this week is no different. Do we have our second softball game? We sure do. Are we still gonna be chest-naked?

Let's not get ahead of ourselves.

Like I said, life keeps on movin' forward, and there's a celebration in town. A party, actually.

It's a birthday party, to be more specific. And, to be even more specific, it's a birthday party for a turtle.

You heard me. Our town is throwin' a birthday party for a turtle. You're probably thinkin' that it must

43

be a pretty special turtle if the entire town is throwin' a birthday party for it. And, well, our town sure seems to think so.

So, there was a fella in his nineties, Thomas Sturgell, who would always tell this story that when he was a boy of about seven years old, he found a big turtle in town. In his little seven-year-old mind, he decided that he should carve his name in the back of this turtle's shell. He didn't get around to carvin' his full name, but he did manage his initials, TS, right into the shell of that turtle.

Now, you may think that people would say, "Show us this amazin' turtle that you have beheld." But they didn't.

They said, "Thomas, why in the world did you carve your initials into the shell of this turtle, you senseless boy?"

They told him that carvin' his initials into the turtle's shell would kill it. Well, as the story goes, Thomas felt awful. He went home and cried because he was sure he must have killed that turtle.

Fast-forward here recently in town, a big ol' turtle was found walkin' near Chet Dilroy's property outside of town, and Chet noticed a curious etchin' on his back. Not Chet's back. The turtle's back.

And so, Chet steps closer and sees the initials TS on this turtle's shell. Well, Chet, like most folks in this area, has heard this story. And Thomas Sturgell told the story 'til he died, and the older he got, the crazier folks thought he was.

Now we got some figurin' to do. And that's exactly what town officials did. How old was Thomas Sturgell when he died? And how old did he say he was when he found that turtle? And let's say it was so many years when he found it—and then them town officials come up with a number that they could confidently and safely say, "This is about how old that turtle is today."

And what did they conclude? This turtle is 107 years old. And what do you do when you find a 107-year-old turtle? You celebrate. So, there's a town party this week, complete with a birthday song for the turtle.

And I don't know if you have spent much time with turtles, but it can be hard to know what they are thinkin'. But when they start singin' to that turtle, I'm pretty sure he rolls his eyes.

They have a sheet cake for it. Then a limbo contest. The turtle won. He moves slow. And just judgin' by his body language—now, let me be clear, I ain't a turtle-ologist, but from what I could tell—the turtle was underwhelmed by the whole thing. I mean truly not impressed.

Folks took pictures with the turtle. The turtle got a piece of sheet cake, which I think it could've taken or left it. And then they put a party hat on the turtle and released it back to the wild.

I'm almost positive that he hated the party hat. I mean, do we really think that he has a place to hang that party hat when he gets home? Do turtles have hat racks? I don't think so. I'm gonna' go out on a limb and say that a 107-year-old turtle does not have a hat rack at home.

So off he went. And you know how when someone visits you—like an aunt or a more likable cousin—and you stand out in the yard and wave as they drive away until they turn the corner? And you're wavin' until they are outta sight?

Well, they tried this with the turtle. You know how long it takes for a 107-year-old turtle to walk across the lawn at the community center in town? I mean, a while. Finally, Ricky Don Pierson loaded it in his F-250—Ricky Don's a volunteer firefighter—and took that turtle back out near the pond north of Chet Dilroy's property, else folks would still be wavin'.

Cheryl Grubbs got a cramp in her tricep from wavin' that turtle off. I mean, they kept it up a few minutes before Ricky Don called it.

Sheet cake and party hat? Come on.

So, imagine an event like that for Myron Curtis, who's fresh in love with Mary Beth Tucker, and he's in charge of our softball team uniforms.

I stop by the Burger Shed after the turtle party and before the softball game. And who is there? Cricket. I know that has to be her inside talkin' to Bud. Now is my chance. I lean my bike against the wall outside just as Mort Dwydell leaves with a bag of food.

"You ready for tonight, Tavin?"

"Yeah, Mort."

Now, I'm lookin' past Mort, tryin' to see Cricket as she wraps up her conversation with Bud. Mort pulls his sleeve up and shoves his tricep in my face.

"Does this look like a skeeter bite to you?"

"What, Mort?"

I lean back and try to focus on whatever he is showin' me. "A little bit, Mort. Could be."

"Well, I'm tryin' not to scratch it, but I was wonderin' if maybe a fire ant got me and not a skeeter."

As Mort rambles on about his tricep bite, Cricket has made it to her truck and pulls onto Main Street.

And, when it's all said and done, Mort don't need to be itchin' it, whatever bit him.

We show up to the fields this week thirty minutes before game time, and not only do we not see any uniforms, we don't see any Myron.

I know what you are thinkin' . . . *What is Myron thinkin'?*

And, trust me, we are all wonderin' that.

Well, Russell Tucker takes a lap over by the concession stand, and sure enough Myron is leanin' up against the side of the concession stand gigglin' with Mary Beth Tucker. They are really in their own world.

And Russell hollers at him, thinkin' that would snap Myron out of it. You know like, "Myron! It's game time!"

Myron kinda turns toward Russell and smiles. "Okay, Russell. I'll be there directly."

Russell is annoyed, shakin' his head at his sister. "Mary Beth, you might want to get to work in that snack stand before the line gets any longer."

Well, she peeks around and sees the line; now she's embarrassed. She ain't even heated up the nacho cheese yet, which ain't on the menu anyway, but she brought it.

So, Myron makes his way over to the fields with Russell, and then we was all waitin' at the team dugout because we are the visitors again tonight.

If you ain't familiar with local adult league softball, that's how it works. We play at the city fields. There's three softball fields, and the concession stand is in the middle. We ain't never had a league big enough to have all three fields goin' on a game night. Usually kiddos are playin' on one for fun and Little League might have the other.

Our games are usually on Field Three, and the way it's positioned, just on the other side of third base is a little parkin' lot, and then the big parkin' lot is on the other side of our outfield fence—mostly right field.

Just on the other side of the center field wall is a grassy area with hay bales where they have archery classes. Chet Dilroy teaches junior archery out there. He's the one who found that old turtle.

All that to say, everybody in the softball league lives here in town. Which means everybody is always at home. You can't always be the home team. And turns out we are the visitin' team again this week. See how that works? We ain't like the Atlanta Braves and they get to St. Louis and say, "Well, we are the away team because that sign says St. Louis, not Atlanta. We gotta be in the away team dugout."

Every week in our league you are showin' up at home. So, you gotta ask the ump or check your schedule to see where you are supposed to be. And we are in the away dugout again tonight.

As Myron approaches, I see the color drain from his face. He's lookin' at all of us waitin'—except for Brodie Childress. Brodie had to fix a hole in the floorboard of his Suzuki Sidekick. It wasn't a new hole, but his toddler lost a shoe out the bottom today and they went back later and couldn't find it. So, he was hopin' to make it to the field at some point durin' the game.

We ain't got a sub on our team. So, if somebody is missin', we down a man. So . . . we're down a man until Brodie gets that floorboard patched.

But, why is Myron so alarmed, you ask? Well, he sees all of us in the shirts we wore to the fields and I think that triggers him to remember somethin'. You know where I'm goin' with this?

Do you even wanna know?

For the second week in a row, Myron forgot our uniforms. So, our team pulls off our shirts for week two as skins. And we also decided to bench Myron because he has given his word two weeks in a row now and failed both times. So, he's chest-naked wearin' tight sweats and a fanny pack in our dugout.

He's on our team, so he's gotta be dressed out. Now we're down two guys. We're takin' the field with seven players. That's me—Tavin Dillard—Mort Dwydell, Russell Tucker, Rance Farnhart, Rusty Tidwell, Cody Briggs, and JT Whitlow.

JT lives in my trailer park too. We workin' on puttin' together a zip line between our trailers.

But tonight we are chest-naked again and battin' first. Russell Tucker has put together the lineup, but he has to shuffle it around a bit because of the missin' players. The team ain't happy with Myron.

I'm hot, buddy. I'm thinkin' how can this guy get so caught up in his new gal and a turtle party that he forgets our uniforms two weeks in a row? Well, who cares now; he did forget, and here we are.

If you've ever played sports and you've gone into a game knowin' you are shorthanded and probably worse than the other team, then you kinda know what we are dealin' with. It's like if you walk into a PE class and you see some of the kids warmin' up and they doin' things you think you are supposed to know, but you thinkin', *I just got here. I'm here to learn. I ain't showin' up ready to go pro.* It can be a little bit of a gross feelin'.

But, we're full-growed men, and we got a game to play. And we ain't makin' excuses, but we are makin' sure that Myron Curtis ain't in charge of the uniforms from here on out.

It's the top of the first. Russell has me battin' third, but after he shuffled the lineup, I'm battin' lead off. I stand in, still thinkin' about bein' chest-naked. I'd like to say what happened next was me readin' the game, improvisin', respondin' in the moment, but really I was steady zoned out and daydreamin'.

They tossed that slow pitch softball up in the air.

Donnie Wayne Chambliss is on the other team. He's a couple years younger than me. In grade school, he got really into squirrels.

He had so many pet squirrels growin' up that his daddy finally stopped squirrel huntin' because of the fits Donnie Wayne would throw. His daddy ended up huntin' a bunch of rabbit, hogs, and deer—you know he kinda doubled down on the others. When Donnie Wayne finally moved out, his daddy went to town on them squirrels.

I mean after years thinkin' they was in a safe zone, them squirrels got comfortable, and Mr. Chambliss got out there and took his yard back. Donnie Wayne didn't talk to his dad for five months, but by the time Thanksgivin' rolled around he knew he wanted to eat his momma's cookin' and they was talkin' again.

So, this is the ol' boy tossin' the pitch, Donnie Wayne. Before I know it, that ball drops on my front right foot—because I'm a lefty. And they give me first base.

The way they say it is that they award you first base. You been awarded. You get an award. Sure makes you feel like you really went out and accomplished somethin'.

But truth be told, I was daydreamin'. I'm awake now. And I can't stay on one base long. And Donnie Wayne will toss that pitch so high, you could somersault all the way to second and steal it attaway. So, there wadn't no way I was gonna try and stay on first long.

Mort Dwydell is up next. He takes the first pitch, and I'm off. Headfirst, Pete Rose, chest-naked into second base. Gravel, pebbles, dirt, and a raw chest. Safe.

I'm pretty sure what just happened was impressive, but Mort hollers at me from the batter's box.

"It's the first innin', Tavin! Give me a chance to hit!"

I said, "Here's your chance, Mort! I didn't take no bat outta your hand!"

Him and that tricep skeeter bite can just mess around and hit a dinger as far as I'm concerned.

"Just stay put!" Mort hollers. He's tryin' to be a base runnin' coach, but all he needs to worry about is puttin' a hurtin' on that ball. We wasn't tryin' to, but I think we got in the other team's head because we was yellin' at each other. Well, Donnie Wayne go to toss that next pitch, and I'm off!

I ain't got no business standin' at second when I could be standin' at third. Well, Mort swings, and that thing is launched. It sails well over the center field wall, right up against a hay bale. Mort took a stolen base away from me, but that homer scored two, and we was winnin' quick.

Myron Curtis is standin' in the dugout clappin'. Everybody is pretty pumped up. We got a couple more in the first thanks to JT Whitlow and Rusty Tidwell.

JT got to second on an overthrow to first base that rolled up next to Cheryl Grubbs's husband, Shane. He's out with his metal detector. I mean, that man will do more damage to a lawn than an army of moles. He's got a little garden shovel—that metal detector beeps, and three minutes later he's diggin' up a bottle cap to put in his little treasure satchel.

So, that ball rolls up to his foot, and he kinda kicks it away. I guess cause it ain't metal and he ain't got no interest in it. But anyhow, JT got second base.

They don't let Shane get on the fields to metal detect. I heard he does anyway, but he puts the ground back. I guess he found a Civil War horseshoe once and some other stuff. He don't play softball. He's a metal detector athlete.

After JT was awarded second base, Rusty Tidwell wasted no time launchin' a two-run shot just over the left field fence.

Softball is funny. If you had seen us play that first innin', you'd say we was about to score thirty runs tonight. Well, we scored five, and Donnie Wayne's Team—Guthrie's Huntin' Supply—scored thirteen. And that's how that went.

The only other RBI we got was when Brodie Childress showed up in the top of the fifth innin' in his Sidekick and hit an opposite field single with Rance Farnhart on third.

Myron Curtis stayed in the dugout, chest-naked and clappin' all night. I will say this. He didn't complain about bein' benched. He took it and supported the team. But that don't mean we countin' on him to bring them uniforms next week. After the game I'm gettin' a Dr Pepper from the concession stand, and me and Russell asked him where he ordered the uniforms from. We'll get 'em picked up this week.

Myron looks at the ground like a toddler with a cheek full of stolen Snickers Bar, and he don't say nothin'. Russell says, "Myron, which uniform place did you go to?"

In my head I'm thinkin', there's only two places in our tri-county area that do this, so we could guess and have a fifty-fifty chance, but why won't Myron just speak up?

Then Myron looks up at us and says, "Guys, I never did order them uniforms."

Come again? Are you tellin' me we been chest-naked for two weeks thinkin' our uniforms were sittin' at a shop waitin' for pickup and they ain't even been ordered? Our uniforms don't even exist?

Myron shrugs. "Sorry, guys. I forgot."

Russell says, "Where's the money?" Myron unzips his fanny pack and looks through it. "I think it's still in here."

Sure enough, he pulls out our uniform money. I take it and tell the team that I'll take care of it this week. I mean, two weeks into softball season and we oh-and-two and chest-naked. I got road rash up my chest, and we ain't even got a sponsor or a team name. Well, we might not win next week, but we are gonna have uniforms, I can tell you that much.

So, Mary Beth and Myron were a little more reserved after the game. She had to hand out sno-cones to the winners, Guthrie's, and they ran outta cherry. Stinks for them.

And that's how game two went . . . a little like game one, chest-naked and we lost. But, fool me twice and I won't show up chest-naked three weeks in a row. Especially if I keep stealin' bases.

Our nameless team didn't have a great week. I got one step closer to sayin' hey to Cricket. That 107-year-old turtle is probably havin' a better week now that folks ain't singin' to him, puttin' a party hat on him, and feedin' him sheet cake.

Funny, ain't it? He ain't got a uniform and he don't want one. Our team needs uniforms and we ain't got 'em. And, truth be told, a piece of sheet cake don't sound so bad to me right about now.

4

SHIRTS

You ain't gotta be an Alvin Einsteins[4] to know things have not started well this softball season. You know that. I know that. The whole town seems to know that. If you're like me, when you face a situation you don't really care for, you try to figure out how to make it better. So, how do we make this season better?

Firstlys, it'd be nice to field a full team. We was down one and a half players last week. Myron Curtis got benched for not pickin' up our uniforms for the second week in a row. Brodie Childress didn't show up 'til the fifth innin'.

---

4. Editor's note: Albert Einstein, theoretical physicist.

So, Myron was there, but he had to sit the bench, chest-naked like the rest of us. Bein' skins is fine for some front yard football when you're in elementary school, but we are older than that. Way older.

And to add insalt to injury, Myron informs us that there ain't no uniforms to pick up. They ain't even there he says. Turns out Myron can't focus on much more than a couple things at a time, and between his new girlfriend, the town's birthday party for a 107-year-old turtle, and softball season launchin', he dropped the ball. His head is in the clouds ever since he started datin' Mary Beth Tucker.

After I got the uniform cash from Myron, I put on my thinkin' cap.

Now, lotsa teams in the league have sponsors. Lonnie Brunwell's team, Brunwell Tires, is sponsored by his daddy's shop, Brunwell's Tires. And Team Sonic, well they sponsored by Sonic. Last week we got beat by Guthrie's Huntin' Supply. Now, we didn't have no sponsor, so Myron said he was just gonna pick out some generic green uniforms, and that'll be that.

We've had a week to figure this out. So, I've been figurin'. Then a light bulb dings. You know how a light bulb goes on when you are thinkin' and it kinda dings, like, *hey, that's an idea.* And sure enough, turns out it was an idea.

So, I put on my bike ridin' shoes. Which is like my regular shoes, but I ride my bike while I'm wearin' them. And I rode that bike all the way to Bud's Burger Shed in town.

I bet you see where this is goin', don't ya? I mean, there ain't no twists and turns in this story. It's a straight shot. I thought about Bud's Burger Shed, and I ran it by Russell Tucker and Mort Dwydell. "How about I ask Bud if he would sponsor our team?"

We got an envelope full of money, and we're all tired of bein' chest-naked. The math seems to add up to me. I mean, I ain't no math-ologist, but I tell ya we all thought that sounded right.

So, I arrive at the Burger Shed to talk to Bud. He's a good businessman. As a small business owner myself, runnin' my lawn care service, I know a little about business, and Bud, he can run that thing. Now, he's a little old school, so if you think he can Door-Dash you a number three combo meal, well that ain't gonna happen. Come on in and slide into a booth, go through the drive-thru, or send your little brother in on his bike to pick it up.

Bud makes a great burger, and his new onion ring recipe finally solved them woes. That last recipe he was tryin' to use was not workin'. Them rings would crack like mud on the hood of a Chevy S-10 with a lift kit, and once you bite into it, that breadin' cracks and falls everywhere. You try to bite into that onion, and now it's gettin' pulled out all slimy like an alligator gar[5] in an irrigation ditch. Did not work. But he switched it up.

All that to say, Bud don't like change, but he has tried new stuff and it's worked out. It's closer to two p.m. I took a late lunch because I knew I wanted to chat sponsorship with him, and I wanted him to be able to sit and talk. And Bud don't sit durin' the lunch rush—he'll stand at your table and talk, but he just don't sit while it's that busy.

So, he slides in across from me at the Burger Shed, and I told him, "I wanna talk to you about the Burger Shed sponsorin' a softball team."

Bud is pretty good at landin' the plane, so he says, "What exactly does that mean?" I'm about to answer his question when he asks, "Is your team any good?"

"I'm glad you asked, Bud. We have had two games, and we played chest-naked. I can show you the road rash from stealin' bases headfirst these last two weeks."

Bud quickly declined that offer, and I said, "We

---

5. *Editor's note: An alligator gar is the largest freshwater fish in North America.*

got a lotta heart—or a pretty good amount of heart. A lot may be an overstatement."

"So you stink?"

"Now, Bud, hear me out. We was down one and a half players last week."

I go on to explain how we are havin' to deal with some commitment and focus issues. Most of us are lookin' at this as a serious commitment. It's on our schedule. We even look forward to it durin' the week. We show up early. We on a team. It's fun.

Then there's the Brodie Childresses of the world, who don't always bother to call, but a week later they say, "Oh, my wife made her famous three bean salad that night, and I stayed home to eat it. It's better fresh."

I'm thinkin' ain't half of three bean salad vinegar? That means them beans should keep for fifty years, but that's the kinda things he says. Or maybe somethin' came up. Like last week he had to get the hole patched in the floorboard of his Suzuki Sidekick.

And that's how we was down one and a half players last week.

Bud leans forward, interested like he was thinkin'. And then he said, "Did the Childress boy really miss a game for three bean salad?"

I shook my head and said, "Not this season, Bud . . . So, you wanna know what a sponsor is gonna do?"

Bud nods. "What in the world do you need from me, Tavin?"

"Bud, we need uniforms. So, firstly, I would say that we need Bud's Burger Shed shirts. And then this would mean our team name would be Bud's Burger Shed. Maybe Team Burger Shed. Somethin' like that."

Bud says, "That's kind of a long name."

"Well, I didn't name your restaurant, Bud!"

He nods. "Okay, you can buy my shirts."

Then, I slid the envelope of cash across the table to Bud and said, "So do we get free food or anything?"

He shakes his head and says, "No, I don't think so."

So, I nod. Fair enough. He did say he'd pass along coupons every now and then. Seemed like a win to me. We got shirts; he even had sizes big enough for Myron and Mort. Russell's a big boy too, but he's tall, not just wide. Myron and Mort are well under that.

The shirts are comfy, and they advertise my favorite place to eat, *and* I don't have to play chest-naked this week. Or should I say I *didn't* have to play chest-naked this week. That's right.

I was just about to ask Bud about the produce

delivery schedule, but his phone rang and he was off. I figured I should be too.

It's game three, and we show up to the fields officially as Team Burger Shed. We was not chest-naked. I repeat: We ain't chest-naked. Felt like a win already.

Myron Curtis ain't benched anymore. So, we have him back. Now, Brodie Childress, that's another story. He and his wife had gone outta town to the outlet mall, and that took longer than he thought it would.

He's tellin' me in the dugout durin' the third innin' when he finally got there that they had gone to them outlets and his wife wanted a pair of long pants. And they went to Adracandle and Flanch.[6] Apparently they sell them breeches she wanted there.

Brodie said, "Tavin, I could buy two gently worn tires for the front end of my Suzuki Sidekick for the amount of money them long pants cost."

I said, "You gotta be kiddin' me."

He said, "I ain't. And then she wanted a handbag, so she wanted to look at Versnotchy.[7] And she seen them prices and was like, 'We can't do this.' I mean, she likes to shop, but she seen them Versnotchy prices

---

6. *Editor's note: We could not locate this store.*
7. *Editor's note: This one either.*

and pumped the brakes on that because it was so high dollar."

And I asked, "Did y'all go to one of them sit-down places?"

And he said they weren't gonna do that, but he took her to a burrito place, and they got big ol' burritos, the size of a full-growed wild rabbit—the ones with the longer haunches.

He said he cut that burrito in half with a plastic knife, and they shared it. But they made a whole day and a half of it at the outlet malls. That sounded 'spensive for one pair of pants. I told Brodie I hope them trousers can do the laundry, make the bed, and change the oil on that Sidekick for the price they paid. He was like, "I wish they did!"

So, here we are in the third innin' of our third game. We oh-and-two, but the good news is, we ain't like one of them high school football teams you hear about that ain't won in three or four years. You know them ones that ain't even scored a point in that amount of time. We have scored in our first two games. Made some good contact, but we just couldn't string enough runs together or stop the other team from havin' big innin's. And if you know anything about softball, those are two big keys. Like you gotta do both of them to have any success.

Well, by the third innin' I already realize I was dealin' with a regular Catch Twenty-Three[8]—because, yes, now I have a uniform. And, yes, I ain't gotta steal bases chest-naked and get all ate up by that gravelly infield, but now I got a nice, comfy, sharp-lookin' uniform, and I ain't sure I wanna get it all dirty.

Sounds silly I know. It's like when Memaw bought a cookie jar and said it was just for looks. We couldn't lift the lid. She wouldn't put nothin' inside it. She said it was too pretty to use. I mean, I ain't seen nothin' like it. It had two hummingbirds flappin' they wings by a bush that's got these flowers on it that I guess hummin' birds like. And they are by a clear brook that's flowin'. And a full-growed doe is lappin' water from the brook, and in the sky up high is a bald eagle. Then the lid of the cookie jar is painted like the sky with a few little clouds, but mostly just a clear, sunny day.

So, you can see why she'd want that handled with care, but not to be handled at all? Well, now all of a sudden I knowed how Memaw felt about that cookie jar as I sit in the dugout at the softball fields in my Bud's Burger Shed shirt. You may be wonderin'

8. *Editor's note: We believe this to actually be a sophisticated, if misidentified, literary allusion.*

if these shirts would hold up to the rigors of an adult league softball game.

Well, I can do ya one better and tell you they held up to the rigors of Myron Curtis—softball or no softball. Now, the reason I'm in the dugout talkin' with Brodie Childress is because we are battin', and if you know anything about softball, you bat one person at a time. You can't send more than one person up there.

Myron steps on an aluminum bat on the way out the dugout to the batter's box. His shoulder slams against the chainlink exit gate of the dugout, and he loses his footin'. There ain't no catchin' him; you just gotta get out of the way.

Now, I don't know if Myron was thinkin' through all the responses to accidents in his head as he was fallin', but he sure enough turns his shoulder so his back took most of the impact, and then he tries to roll outta that fall and pop up like he meant to do it. Well, he's got the will, but he does not have the leg or arm strength to catapult that frame of his to the standin' position.

He gets partial off the ground, gravity takes over, and his little feet are movin' like them fellas at the stunt shows that run on them spinnin' logs in the water. And then his hands go out because that's what hands do when you about to fall. They reach out to catch ya. Well, he topples back to the ground. His sweat breeches lost a little ground around the waist, and Myron put on a little show, much like a plumber would underneath your sink.

And all that to say, his Team Burger Shed shirt hit a chain-link dugout fence then the ground about three times with the full weight of Myron behind the impact before he comes to rest on his back like a box turtle that lost its balance tryin' to climb over a decorative patio brick.

It's quite a picture, and that shirt held up. Myron makes it to the batter's box eventually and promptly lays into that softball for a pop fly out. Even after all of that, I'm not really wantin' to mess up this shirt.

Somethin' about goin' two weeks chest-naked that made me forget how to be aggressive with a shirt on. I don't know the whole psychology behind that, but I was not a terror on the base paths this week as I've been known to be. I did steal third on my breeches in the fifth innin' just legs first. Didn't feel right since I'm a headfirst, Pete Rose kinda guy.

I got stranded at third base that innin', and here we are game three, they scored seven runs, and we pushed two across. So, quick math will tell ya that we are oh-and-three.

Now that score don't tell you the intangibles, like we played with a little more dignity tonight thanks to not bein' chest-naked. That was a big deal.

And we fielded our whole team from the fourth innin' on. You ain't gotta be a genius to know that is a beautiful thing.

5

DINNER ROLLS

Rance Farnhart runs the Bait and Tackle Shop. He has for a long time. His folks, Jerry Don and Cybil Farnhart, run the flea market in town. So, Rance comes by that business sense honest.

And he knows how to give haircuts. Where, Tavin? Out at the Bait and Tackle Shop, on the patio. And it ain't just haircuts and bait and tackle out there. He's got a restaurant—real good fish and chips—where folks eat on the patio.

So, he's gotta plan that right. He gets them haircuts done on the patio either before or after the lunch rush. You can't have folks eatin' out there with Rance just sweepin' hair while they munchin' down on fish and chips.

Reason how come I say all this is because Brodie Childress was not late this week. Why? He needed a haircut. And you know where he went? That's right. And Rance ain't late for softball games.

Brodie went there for a haircut today, and Rance brought him to the game all cleaned up. I mean, Brodie had Rance leave some length in the back, but that's on purpose.

It was only two weeks with no uniforms, but it sure felt like longer. Now we got uniforms, and it feels like we are movin' in the right direction. Once you look around and see a bunch of guys that have the same shirt as you—it feels like y'all belong, like a team.

I mean, truth be told, when we was playin' chest-naked and I looked around, we didn't look like *oh, they wearin' the same uniform.*

We was all wearin' special-made uniforms—if you know what I mean—courtesy of McDonald's burgers and fries, Burger Shed milkshakes, tots with cheese from Sonic—I mean that kinda thing. Bodies-built-by-fast-food-skins. So, at least that's behind us.

We are playin' the city workers this time. PJ Mc-Gee mows the city fields, and he got some fellas he works with to be a team. Team Burger Shed may not be a team of all-stars, but I feel like we are as ready as we've ever been today. Rusty Tidwell is sayin' the same thing.

Myron Curtis, his head is still in the clouds. He gets a hit in the second innin', and he's roundin' first and decides to blow a kiss to Mary Beth Tucker. I guess she was standin' outside the concession stand; otherwise she wouldn't be able see him.

I can't believe it. Just when I think Myron is turnin' a corner, he turns toward second base and eats it. He falls hard. Steady puttin' that shirt to the test this week too.

He gets throwed out from deep left field because he's lyin' in the base path like a toddler makin' a snow angel, 'cept he ain't movin'. He's kinda stunned.

I'm thinkin', *Myron, don't be blowin' kisses roundin' first base. Don't be doin' that.*

Insalt to injury, Myron disappears in between innin's. Where'd he go? We don't wanna send one of our teammates to go find him because we got a game to play, so I ask my brother Bret to go get him.

I never know when I'm gonna see my brother. He comes and goes—he don't live in town no more. I really ain't sure where he lives. But I seen him tryin' to sell a broken remote control dump truck to a nine-year-old and holler to him, askin' if he could find Myron. I told him to let Myron know he needs to get back over to the fields. He's gonna bat soon.

Well, I don't know how your brother is, but my brother needs to know what's in it for him.

So, that's exactly what he asks, "What's in it for me, Tavin?"

"I don't know, Bret. You can use the good card table to wrestle."

His eyes are wide because he loves to wrestle in the trailer park when he comes around. And I won't let him use the one good card table we have to top rope them opponents. A grown man jumpin' off a good card table to land on somebody wrestlin' turns it into a bad card table pretty quick.

He snatches a ten-dollar bill from the kiddo and shoves that broken dump truck into the boy's hands, then he hauls tail to find Myron. No rhyme or reason that I could tell. No strategy, just runnin' and hollerin'. "Myron! Myron Curtis! Where'd you go? Don't you know you got a softball game to play?"

Bret turns the corner, and there's Myron leanin' into the window of the concession stand, kinda gigglin' and eatin' what appeared to be a hot dinner roll.

Why there is a hot dinner roll at the concession stand, I did not know. I could only guess.

My best guess is, let's say you workin' at a concession stand and you on your way to the fields to work. You're hungry. You pick up a meal on the way. It's in one of them styrofoam close-me-down boxes. And in that box along with whatever meal you ordered there is a dinner roll. That's my best guess at how a hot buttered dinner roll could end up at the concession stand and in Myron Curtis's hand at the softball fields.

Well, Bret's got his attention—I mean he's workin' for that good card table. It wadn't 'til later that I started to regret this offer. When you are in the middle of a battle on the softball field, there's a lot a man might say to make sure his entire team is on the field and ready to play.

And it turns out Myron was really enjoyin' that dinner roll, which I assumed came from a to-go meal at some eatery nearby. I was wrong.

Bret decides to hold Myron by the collar even though he is already headin' back our way. I guess just to show me that he is the one who caught him. Like a bounty hunter, and he wants everybody to know not only did this fella get caught, but he was caught by Bret Dillard. So, that's how that works, best I can tell.

Myron is kinda wide-eyed like a toddler who is unawares he's even in trouble. Which, for an adult actin' that way, can be borderline infuriatin'. Myron walks toward me and shows me his elbow.

"What is that, Myron?"

"It's a Band-Aid for my injury."

I kid you not, Myron got a little scuff hittin' that infield and had Mary Beth put him on a Band-Aid. C'mon, Myron. You seen my chest? That's road rash from two weeks of chest-naked headfirst slides. So, don't even get me started on injuries.

At least it wadn't no Pokemon or little kid Band-Aid. It was just a regular one.

"They had dinner rolls over there that was softer than a baby angel's leg, Tavin. And plenty of butter too."

How's that?

"Mary Beth made her momma's recipe and brought a batch to the concession stand, and she's sellin' 'em."

Now, I ain't never had no baby angel's leg—I imagine nobody has, but the way Myron described that, it put it together in my head in such a way that made me think, that's a pretty soft roll.

"Oh, they slide right down, Tavin."

"We got a game to play, Myron, and I can't have

you blowin' kisses, gettin' Band-Aids, and eatin' baby angel leg dinner rolls."

"With butter!" Myron says.

"Whatever, Myron! We can't be doin' that. This is softball season. We already oh-and-three, and you gotta get your head outta the clouds. You gotta!"

Now, we up to bat, and Rusty Tidwell plays ball like he does anything else—locked in. I mean, that guy can have a good time just hangin' at the river, on a rope swing, back flips and all that. But even then, he's locked in. Can't nobody have focused fun like Rusty. He just got a mind for that I guess. And on top of all that focus, he's an athlete. When it comes to adult softball, them can be few and far between—just like Mort Dwydell and milk.

Mort can't have no dairy, but it's rare that he don't try and sneak somethin' in. He's got that thing where it'll tear up his guts if he has ice cream, milkshakes, cheese, or butter. It's that *Maltose Apology*. Which is like Cajun for no milk, I think. That might not be the name . . . it's *Milktrate Refugee*, *Maltate Rosary* where you can't get into no dairy. *Milktrap Bahadgeny*. [9]

He told me his wife will take the kids and head to a

---

9. *Editor's note: Lactose intolerance. Apologies to Mr. Dwydell for the public release of his private medical information.*

hotel or her momma's for the weekend because he will tear up the whole house down into the garage. He said it even soured the carport, even though it's open air.

So, Rusty steps up to bat, and he don't have no strategy except to knock the cover off that ball. And that's what he does. He launches that thing over the left field wall. Cindy Mydell is out there walkin' her dog. It's a retired firehouse dog, and she tried to pass it off one time as a seein' eye dog at a Walmart's Rollback sale where I was workin' volunteer police. But it ain't no seein' eye dog.

It's only got one eye! The whole reason it was retired was A, it was old, and secondly, because it got in a fight with a squirrel and lost an eye. So, she tried to say a one-eyed retired firehouse dog was a seein' eye dog. She got busted. Let's just say that. Not on my volunteer police watch, Cindy. No ma'am.

Rusty's homer rolls out to that dog, and I don't guess it ain't got no periphery—especially outta that eye that don't work—and that ball rolls up to its foot, and that thing jumps and yanks the leash loose from Cindy Mydell, and then it turns and starts attackin' that softball.

Now, we ain't like the major leagues where you catch a foul ball and you got yourself a souvenir. I don't know about your town, but 'round here, you bring a homer ball or foul ball back to the concession stand, you can trade that thing for a free sno-cone.

So, Cindy's one-eyed dog is puttin' a hurtin' on that softball. Bitin' it, slobberin' all over it. It's a mess. It finally starts gettin' the cover off.

I'm thinkin', *I hope she don't think she gettin' a free sno-cone for that thing. If anything, just a cup of ice, because we ain't gonna be able to use that ball now.*

Well, sticky fingers Cindy just picks up that nasty ball, drops it in her handbag, and keeps it. So, that's how that went. Rusty's home run ball met quite an end. But that put us within one run of the other team.

I get on first with a squibber down the third base line. I love to slide but went in feet first. Good thing too, because that sweep tag the first baseman tried woulda hit me in the face. All he had to do at first was catch it. He ain't gotta tag me. I don't know if he's tryin' to send me a message, but in the end I think he got a message from me.

Hello. Look who's standin' on first base. And then Rance Farnhart pops out to the catcher. And the innin' kinda peters out from there.

The rest of the game we didn't get much else goin'.

We have some good news and bad news from the fields this week. Myron was locked in the rest of the game. That's the good news.

Bad news is we lost again. This time it was three to two, and to a casual passerby who may have caught an innin' or two of the game, they might say, "Hey, that team over there? That Burger Shed team is semi-competitive."

And, in my book, that's a win at this point. To play to a three-two score is pretty noble. Honestly, once Myron mentioned them dinner rolls, everybody's head was out of it. The team made a beeline over there after the game to get one. Sold out fast.

I didn't even get one of them rolls. And I have no idea if they are gonna be at the concession stand next week. In my mind, I'm thinkin', *just stick to sno-cones, hot dogs, sodas, and Skittles, Mary Beth.* She's bringin' hot buttered dinner rolls softer than a baby angel's leg on a whim. Folks ain't gonna know what to expect every week—not to mention they can't even keep all the sno-cone flavors in stock.

I think we are gettin' close. I really do. It's only a matter of time, and things will turn. That's just how life works. You crank at somethin' long enough, you bound to get some results. Sometimes somebody cranks at somethin' for ten minutes or two innin's and hopes for ten years or one season's worth of results. Nope, crank that for years, and you might get that pump primed, and you seein' results for decades to come.

Now, we just tryin' to win next week. And we are due. Not because of all our losses, but because we are puttin' in the work.

I didn't really have time to sulk over losin' a soft-ball game or losin' out on Mary Beth Tucker's dinner rolls that were softer than a baby angel's leg.

I seen Rusty Tidwell's wife, and she was tellin' him that the new girl is coverin' a shift for her down at the nursin' home. New girl? I asked what her name was, and Rusty's wife told me her name is Cricket. Well, well, well. Looks like when I'm ready to say hi, I know where to find her.

I ain't got no time now because I have to let my brother Bret use the good card table for some trailer park wrestlin'. He wants to top rope elbow drop and do all of that. It don't take long for a crowd to gather, and I about got caught up in it.

Truth be told, I did get caught up in it. Because anytime I have the opportunity to go head-to-head with my older brother, buddy, it's on. He tries to top rope me, but I get him with the ground game. Tied him up with a figure four leg lock; he tries to reverse it. No luck.

But before I even got into it with him, I took that shirt off because I still ain't used to havin' a uniform. Even though it's for wearin', I took it off to whoop my brother. I'm just gonna save it for game nights right now.

That card table lasts a little bit longer than a remote control car does. Remote control cars last about eleven seconds once they get fired up. And that card table lasts upwards forty seconds before a leg snapped on it. Then Bret picks it up to whack JT Whitlow, who blocks it with the top of the card table. The rules got a little loose as the night went on. It turns into a street fight, and eventually Bret is picked up by the police. Then things get quiet.

Say what you want about my brother, but he got Myron back to the fields, and that's what I asked him to do.

For the week ahead, I've got my eye on our first W of the season. We ain't no quitters. I wish Mary Beth Tucker was though. She needs to quit tryin' to mess with the menu at the concession stand.

Or at least bring enough softer-than-a-baby-angel's-leg hot buttered dinner rolls for everybody.

S'MORES

I am a fan of barbecues. I do like to cook a steak or burger on the grill. So, I can't say I'm mad at fire.

You know Hank Thistle's got a burn pile in town goin' year round. I wouldn't want that. Too much pressure to make sure it ain't leaped into a neighbor's yard or what not.

Speakin' of fire. The only fire Team Burger Shed has so far this season is firin' Myron Curtis from bein' in charge of gettin' our uniforms. And now we got a fire lit under us, and we ready to win. I wish I could tell ya that was the only fire at the softball fields this week, but I just can't do that.

You know we are full steam ahead into the softball season. We are oh-and-four, but I wouldn't say a solid oh-and-four. That last game we only lost three to two, and I really think we coulda made somethin' happen there.

We didn't. But we coulda. So, this was week three with uniforms. Those first two chest-naked weeks are becomin' a distant memory. The scabs on my chest from the early days of the season, stealin' bases headfirst, are all healed up. That's another reason I ain't said hey to that gal yet. I gotta be feelin' a little better.

They don't keep track of stolen bases, but I've got thirteen this season. Reason how come I know is because I do keep track. See, that's how that works. Everybody keeps they own scorecard in life. You probably know how many cars you have owned. Or how many cars you have wrecked. Or how many games of horse you won last week at the city park. We all got our lists.

And me? Well, I've stoled thirteen bases. Did one get called back because they said you can't steal first base? Yes. But did I steal it? Yes. Thirteen beautiful bases. That's my list.

Of course, that's a personal list. And we a team.

And you know what they say in team sports—you wanna get that W. And when you're oh-and-four, you ain't got no W. You just ain't.

That's hard when you're in town and folks ask. They just want the bottom line, you know. How many have y'all won? Well, none. Ouch. Kinda stings a little bit, like a fire ant bite. It ain't gonna lay you up for the day, but you feel it. And it hurts a little.

Same with sales.

"How much does it cost?"

"Well, hear me out. This thing can really simplify your life."

"How much?"

"We also sell an attachment that increases productivity by fifty percent."

"How much?"

"We have an easy payment plan."

"How much?"

"We can give you a free satchel too."

"How much!"

"A million dollars."

Can't do it.

Folks don't wanna hear all that other stuff. Well, we coulda won. Shoulda won. We really *wanted* to win. Now, I don't think the first two or three weeks we wanted to win. I know the first two weeks we just wanted shirts.

Wadn't nobody ready to show off our winter bodies. And ol' Myron Curtis hated it with his new gal watchin' nearby, workin' that concession stand, but it was his fault. He did not get our uniforms.

So, yeah, we oh-and-four.

Way I see it, we got the whole league right where we want 'em. Go ahead and sleep on us, and we will be up in your face like a spiderweb across your bathroom doorway. Where'd that come from? Wadn't there yesterday! That's right. You didn't expect it.

Now you spittin', screamin', pullin' web outta your face. Stay alert. Or don't. But Team Burger Shed is comin' for ya. *Bink Bink.*

I was startin' pitcher this week. I'm a lefty. Don't know if I mentioned that before, but I throw left-handed, bat left-handed. Which I guess is a more thorough definition of a lefty.

Big picture is I throwed a two-hitter.

You did read that correctly. I only gave up two hits.

That right there is the glass half full. Now, both them hits was grand slams. Strike zone really got away from me early. Walked some batters, and they made me pay. That's what good players do.

Only thing is, we ain't so bad. I know I keep sayin' that, but it's the truth, and I was ready to prove that this week. Just not on the mound. Maybe somewhere else.

We thought about benchin' Myron for blowin' kisses at Mary Beth Tucker last week and fallin' past first base because of it and gettin' throwed out. But what good is that gonna do?

Hey, stop flirtin' with your girlfriend durin' the game. Why don't we bench you so you can spend the whole game at the concession stand with her? Nah, that ain't gonna work. So, he was there and kinda ready this game.

I say kinda because it was ten minutes 'til game time and I see him pull in on his moped with a propane tank strapped behind him. I mean, that little bungee cord was strugglin' to hold onto that tank. It's like it was sayin', *hey, I'm the size for strappin' down a bag of sunflower seeds or throw pillows that you picked up for your aunt at the flea market. I wadn't built for no propane tank.*

But that little bungee held on with all its might, and Myron arrived not a moment too soon.

He parks, grabs his glove, and releases that propane tank. The bungee cord just curls up and snaps all at the same time. Not sure how Myron was plannin' to get it home, or maybe it's just supposed to stay at the fields.

So, he shuffles over to the concession stand cradlin' a propane tank like a border collie with a hurt ankle that he's rushin' to the vet. Except it wadn't no doggy, it was Myron's softball-gloved hand underneath a propane tank and his other hand holdin' the top.

I'm talkin' about one of them tanks you use to barbecue with. Unless you're a charcoal person. Then, you are rollin' your eyes at the mention of propane and barbecue. Alls I'm sayin' is Myron is hustlin' one of them small propane tanks over to the concession stand. And it's just about game time.

"Myron, what are you doin'?" I call.

He tries to hold up his glove hand like "Hold on" and then he cracks a smile. That tank slips a little bit so he hurries that glove back under it.

"It's gonna be good, Tavin!"

When Myron says somethin' like that, it really means that it ain't gonna be good. At all.

We are the home team tonight, so we are takin the field first. I'm on the mound, and I do wanna be clear, I don't give up two grand slams in the same innin'. I spread them eight earned runs over two innin's. One thing I don't do when somebody cranks one over the fence on me is bark at 'em. Way I see it, my skill is how I bark. So, if they hit a homer, buddy, they out-skilled me. That's on me.

Now my rotator cuff may have been a little tight, I don't know. But I swung my arm around in a full circle like a windmill or like a third base coach wavin' his guy home. And that swingin' felt a little better, but it wadn't clear. Just part of it.

I work out of a jam in the first innin' only givin' up four and then get back into it in the second innin' givin' up another four. Russell Tucker pulls me after that. I don't blame him. It just ain't my night on the mound.

Mort Dwydell pulls one over the wall in the second, so it's eight-to-one in the third when we load the bases. Rusty Tidwell is up. And that's really who you want up in this situation. Rusty is steady focused.

He is locked in. Always.

The concession stand was havin' quite a night as Team Burger Shed starts puttin' pressure on the other team. You remember that propane tank Myron brought?

Well, it's bein' used in the concession stand. Where, Tavin? Did you say set up safely outside the concession stand?

Oh, no. *Inside* the stand. Now, I did not know this durin' the fourth innin'. I found this out later.

Last week Mary Beth Tucker made hot buttered dinner rolls that was softer than a baby angel's leg, accordin' to Myron. And them rolls had plenty of butter.

Apparently Mary Beth is really branchin' out from the traditional concession stand delights and tryin' new stuff. Tonight it was s'mores. Part of the fun of makin' s'mores is roastin' your own marshmallow. If you ain't never had s'mores before or heard of 'em, let me bring you up to speed real quick.

A s'more is a full length graham cracker folded in half to make the top and bottom like a sandwich. But what's on the sandwich? Well, that chocolate square is like a Hershey bar. It fits right on the graham cracker, and then you roast a marshmallow over the fire and then stick it in the middle of the sandwich.

The roastin' marshmallows, that's where the propane tank comes in.

Apparently, Mary Beth figured she had really thought this thing through. She gave folks sticks, and she had a fire goin' in the concession stand. I don't know how much clearer I can be here. *Mary Beth Tucker had a fire goin' inside the concession stand.*

Maybe you are thinkin' it's a roomy concession

stand. Well, it ain't. It's maybe five feet deep and eight feet wide. And there's a counter where folks pay.

Customers are standin' at the window counter, leanin' over with their stick, and roastin' their marshmallow over the fire inside the concession stand. The fire is inside the concession stand. *Inside.*

If this sounds like a recipe for disaster, well, you ain't wrong at all.

About the time Rusty Tidwell is gonna take his first pitch, there is a scream. All of a sudden, there's a kiddo runnin' with a stick that has a marshmallow, on fire, stuck on the end of it. No big deal. We all been there, but to a kid it seems like a big fire. And, truth be told, this is the first marshmallow fire I'd ever seen at the city fields because, well, we don't ever do s'mores there.

I figure some adult would just help put out that fire. Like, calm down, kiddo.

But, that ain't the problem. Next, I see Mary Beth Tucker runnin' out of the concession stand with a bag of chocolate, her purse, and the cash box.

I wouldn't call Mary Beth swift of foot, but like any of us, she can hoof it when she has to.

The concession stand? In flames. I mean, like bonfire-at-the-river kinda flames. Ricky Don Pierson is nearby—he's a volunteer firefighter—and he starts barkin' orders. We trot off the field and out of the dugouts to make sure folks is okay.

Russell Tucker calls the fire department. Ricky Don takes a hose by the bathrooms and starts to spray down the concession stand.

Myron casually mentions, "I hope that propane tank don't blow."

Heads turn. I remember all of a sudden too. Oh, man. Now, folks that have been creepin' toward the stand to see the excitement start backin' away.

Is it gonna blow?

'Bout that time the fire department shows up, and they douse that thing. It smells like a campfire in a rainstorm over there. That propane tank stays quiet.

Now all heads turn to Mary Beth Tucker, and she tries to explain her s'mores in the concession stand idea. I think it's the first time she said it all out loud where she could hear it too, because the look on her face when she tried to explain it said, "Why in the world did I think this was a good idea?"

Like her mouth didn't say that, but her face did. Her face did real hard like attaway.

Ricky Don asks her, "How'd you get the propane tank here?"

I look over at Myron, and so did Mary Beth. He done strapped that thing to his moped. There was no sense to this whole story, and when you say it all out loud, you just wanna shake your head at the both of 'em.

And that's exactly what folks did.

You know how sometimes you want to say it out loud because you think explainin' it to the other person will help them understand? Everybody knows this ain't a good idea. Includin' Myron and Mary Beth, so we all just let sleepin' dogs lie.

Or burnt concession stands simmer.

However you want to look at it.

So, that leaves us at eight-to-one in the fourth innin'. They are talkin' about callin' the game.

I said, "The fields didn't burn, y'all."

But, they gotta go through stuff and drive a firetruck across the field and bring in a patrol car. And they gotta write notes and ask questions. So, they decide to postpone the game. They don't call it. They postpone it.

I think we have a comeback in us.

So, the next night, they done removed the concession stand and cleared that spot. It ain't much to replace a concession stand when it's just a shack you can bring in with a forklift and set down. I mean, there ain't no runnin' water—them sodeys is in a cooler. I guess the sno-cone ice is too.

And everybody knows them Skittles will keep.

Now we are back the next night, and there is just an empty spot where the new stand is gonna be, and I can't explain what happens next, but I'm gonna try.

If you think Rusty Tidwell was locked in last night, imagine him havin' a night to think about that next at bat. Remember them bases was loaded, so that's how we start.

And, truth be told, Rusty had a fella at work today who said he'd give him a ten percent discount on a truck axle if he signed some agreement. Well, turns out that fella didn't have no authority to offer that discount, and the company ain't gonna honor it. And that's frustration Rusty didn't even have last night, ya see?

So, he's got some real aggression pent up there, and he lay into the first pitch of the night. As he make contact he hollers, "Ten percent!" So you know that scam was still on his mind, and I really don't know if that ball has landed yet.

Now it's eight to five. Rance Farnhart follows that with a double. JT Whitlow hit a dribbler to third base, and the third baseman, KC Dunlap—he's Jasteen's husband—just overthought it. He stumbles on the way to the ball and then basically spikes the ball into the ground like he just scored a touchdown.

So, Rance makes it to third, and JT is safe at first. And then, for the first time in my life I see somebody get hit in the neck with a slow pitch softball.

Myron Curtis.

That thing kinda *ca-dunked* the side of his neck. Then he flicks that right shoulder up by his ear so late. It was the reflex of a sloth with a ping-pong paddle.

Too late, buddy. That ball done got pitched, hit you, rolled up the third base line, and we all movin' on, but Myron, he's jumpin' back now, like, *oh, that stung!* And I don't think anyone thought it stung. We watched it get pitched. It was standard slow. So, he's kinda milkin' this moment. I don't know if he thought he had to convince the ump that he got hit, but it was startin' to turn into a production.

So I just say, "Myron, you all right?"

"I got hit by that pitch!"

I said, "Yeah, I see that. Why don't you go ahead and take first."

He nods, but I still think he wants people to know he's hurt, so he starts to jog down the first base line

with a limp. Then I guess he remembers that nothin'
happened to his leg. So, he puts his hand on his neck.

Thankfully, there is no concession stand for Mary
Beth to peek her head out of to offer Myron a Band-
Aid or somethin' unnecessary like that.

So, he makes it down to first, finally, and Russell
Tucker is up. He don't wait. He cranks the first pitch
to the wall. It sounded loud. And their outfielder
seemed to think it was so deep that he ran to the
wall. Like he was gonna jump and rob a home run.

Then he realizes it's gonna drop about fifteen feet
in front of him. It hits that ground, and our guys are
off to the races. Russell ends up with a double, and
Myron is standin' at third. Now it's eight to seven.

I'm up next. I'm a contact hitter. I spray the ball.
Well, I stay back on the first pitch, and for some reason
Myron Curtis starts runnin' home. I'm frozen like a
deer in headlights.

Why in the world would Myron be tryin' to steal
home right now? He is bearin' down hard toward
home plate, and I finally figure I need to move out
the way.

So, I do, and turns out the other team is just as
surprised as us.

The pitcher ain't even pitched it, and he decides

to throw to third base, because that's where Myron was I guess.

And Myron heads home. I'm tellin' him to get down and slide because that's the only way I know to steal a base, but he don't. He is upright. He steps on home and keeps runnin', but now it's turnin' into more of a shuffle, and he sets his hand on his backside, steady focused on gettin' to the bathroom. Myron's got tender guts.

I mean no high fives, nothin'. Myron's about to mess his breeches. And that's what is goin'. on.

He told me later, "Tavin, either I was gonna mess my pants right there on third base or I was gettin' to a bathroom, and I didn't wanna have this game postponed again."

He's probably right. They would've had to hose off that base and probably spray it with Lysol. And every time I headfirst Pete Rose'd it into third base, I'd probably be a little hesitant to reach out and tap that base.

So, Myron Curtis ties up the game by stealin' home, much to everybody's surprise. Let's just say he was highly motivated.

I hit a single off home plate. Bounces high up there. Russell makes it to third on that one. And then Brodie Childress gets himself a single. He pulls it down the line. And we are ahead nine to eight and go on to win eleven to nine. It took two nights, but Team Burger Shed got our first win! What we didn't get was a sno-cone. Disappointed? A little bit. That win did take the sting outta the sno-cone loss, and I'm hopin' they take IOUs.

Put that in your concession stand and burn it. Sorry. Too soon.

By our next game, the concession stand should be back. Mary Beth Tucker can't bring no propane tank to the concession stand now. They wantin' her to stick to the standards—hot dogs, sno-cones, Skittles, sodey. Hmm, sounds like somebody said that before too.

Don't matter now. We are winners, and the softball fields are about to get a new concession stand. Team Burger Shed is fired up. And the concession stand . . . fired down.

CROWS

Chet Dilroy lives out in the country on a big piece of land. He's lived there a number of years. He's married to Gracie, and she runs Early Bird Gets the Perm with her sister, Dalondra.

Chet and Gracie's son lives in Chancellor Park, which is the trailer park I live in. And he's got a little girl named Candy. She's about eight years old, I reckon. Now, Candy Dilroy, on more than one occasion, has caught a crow.

And when I ask Candy, why in the world did you catch that crow? She just looks up at me and says, "They easy to catch." I really thought she might single-handedly rid our trailer park of crows. Them crows are smart, and they talk to each other. And I know for sure they don't like bein' caught by Candy.

First time it happened I was about to start my workday, and Memaw had just gave me the mission of bringin' her back some special edition sodey pop by the end of the day. So, there is a knock on my door. I open the door, and Candy is just kinda lookin' up at me holdin' a full-growed, very embarrassed, adult crow.

I look at Candy. She look up at me like *Bink Bink*. Then I look down at that crow, and it looks up at me: *Bink Bink*. The first time I heard *Bink Bink* was when I got called down to the Burger Shed by Bud to get somethin' out of his air duct. He knew somethin' was up there, but he didn't know what.

He just says, "Tavin, I know it's alive. I can hear it."

So, in exchange for a number three combo meal, I crawled into this air duct and found myself eye to eye with some sorta pigeon. Apparently it had been released from a weddin' a couple weeks before. Now here it was just *Bink Binkin'* at me.

I crawled toward the pigeon wide-eyed. Didn't wanna spook it. And it was wide-eyed like me. First it shook, like a dog gettin' out of water, and then it just locked in with me. I reach out my hands—I got my hands cupped like I'm tryin' to get a bee out of a swimmin' pool.

And that bird looks at me, and I'm lookin' at him. And then I heard them eyes as he looked at me . . . *Bink Bink.* That thing blinked them eyes and took a step into my hands. I *Bink Bink* back and got him outta there. I don't like them tight spaces. You know when you feel locked in them small spaces? Claustrasaures-Rex,[10] where you can't be closed in or you kinda panic.

But I was motivated by that combo meal. Bud's got them seasoned curly fries along with that bacon double cheeseburger and a Dr. Pepper. And I had to back outta that air duct with the bird all the while not gettin' worked up by how tiny the space was. That's how that Claustrasaurus-Rex works—you really battle them tight spaces.

But I got outta there. And now here I am *Bink Binkin'* at a crow that Candy Dilroy holds on my front porch. I mean, she got both her little hands around that full-growed crow. I don't even know how she knocked on my door. She musta kicked it because there ain't no way she coulda let go of that crow and

---

10. *Editor's note: Claustrophobia, the irrational fear of confined spaces.*

knock on the door without it flyin' away.

So here we are. I'm lookin' down at Candy—*Bink Bink*—"Why'd you catch that crow, Candy?"

"They easy to catch."

I shake my head, and I look at that crow.

We make eye contact, and then it just kinda look at the ground, embarrassed.

I'm thinkin', *this is on you, crow. You got wings.*

That crow just shrugged like, *I know. I hate it too.*

So, then I get an idea. You know about them? Like a light bulb goes on, but it ain't a real light bulb. It's just the idea.

I say, "Candy, you like that bird?"

She says, "I sure do. I was hopin' you'd let me use that box underneath your trailer to keep it in. I'm gonna put a bonnet on it and dress it up so pretty."

Oh, that was news to the crow, because now it's lookin' concerned, like, *please sir, if I can have only one request, I behoove thee to help me get free.*

I don't know why the crow talked in Old English, but that's how I put it together in my head when it was just lookin' up at me after that bonnet news.

So, that light bulb goes on, and I say to Candy, "Why don't you let that thing go. And it'll fly, but if it circle back around here and decides to land in that box, then you know it was meant to be. But you gotta let it go to see if it will fly back."

Boy, that crow perked up like, *you think that might work?*

Hear me when I say that I ain't trained in crowology or nothin' like that, but that bird's mood started to change. I ain't sure where a crow's neck ends and his shoulders start. I do know that it seemed like his shoulders straightened up. The hopeful crow.

And Candy looked down at the crow, then back up to me. "Okay," she said.

Then she let that crow go, and it flew away.

I don't speak crow, but I'm pretty sure it said "thank you" as it flew off. And, at the time I thought, Candy mighta done the whole trailer park a favor because that crow will go tell his friends, "Don't go back there; she'll catch ya and dress ya up in a bonnet."

But I ain't tryin' to tell you about Candy Dilory; I'm just sayin' that's the relation because really my story is about her granddaddy, Chet Dilroy.

Now Chet is the one whose property backs up to Rusty Tidwell's, and there's a creek kinda right between 'em. Me and Rusty are workin' on a ramp for remote-control cars that we are gonna be rampin' over the creek at his brother-in-law's birthday party.

Well, Chet's sister-in-law Dalondra had no business bein' on some early-model two-stroke Yamaha moped. She's gunnin' that thing across a field. And I hear it first. Then I see it! I'm thinkin' this ain't gonna be good because she is just haulin' tail across the field, not slowin' down at all.

The thing you gotta remember if you tryin' to ramp a creek on a vehicle like a moped is that you need to have some arm strength because you gotta pull up on the front end of that thing to clear the creek and land it on the other side.

You need a ramp if you tryin' to clear a creek. Well, there ain't no ramp other than one we are about to build for a little remote-control thing. Not a heavyset adult on a standard moped.

Gravity matters. You gotta take that into account. And Dalondra ain't. She's to the edge of the creek, and gravity takes over. The front end went down, and she's smackin' right into the side of the bank, but momentum flipped her over them handle bars.

She Mary Lou Retton'd into the field, like somersault, somersault, stand up. She's kinda worried and scared, but she was okay. I think she was embarrassed too. She should be—kinda senseless what she did.

So, that's Chet Dilroy's sister-in-law. And Chet Dilroy, he teaches junior archery to the youngins on the other side of the center field fence at the softball fields. And they had class this week durin' our game.

Does that matter? Oh, it matters.

Here we are comin' off our first win of the season. It was not an easy win. Hard fought, as they say. The game started, the concession stand caught fire, the next night we finished the game, and we put together a big fat W. You know all that.

We are ridin' high. We went to Bud's afterward and told him the news. We are winners. It was a hoot. Mort Dwydell felt so good he went ahead and celebrated with a milkshake. And he paid dearly for it later, the way he tells it. I really wadn't gonna mine for many details about that. Mort's liable to disclose more than enough when you least expect it—like the middle of the lunch rush at the Burger Shed.

The short story is: Mort has that Milktrape Bahadgeny[11] where he can't have no dairy. It tears him up.

But we did win a game, and he had a week to recover. Of course, I don't know what he did the next day for work. But if I ask, he'll tell me. So, I ain't askin'.

---

11. *Editor's note: Still lactose intolerance.*

Mary Beth Tucker rode a horse to the ball fields tonight. She went to school for horses. She works at a veterinary for her main job. The concession stand is just her job to kinda help out, and now that she's datin' Myron Curtis, she got another reason to be down at the fields.

And I got a reason to show up at the nursin' home. It might sound weird, but I'm tryin' to see if I can get a contract cuttin' their lawn. There's a gal down there I'm ready to see, too. I just gotta figure out what to say to her. But right now I got softball to think about.

The new concession stand has been delivered. It ain't painted yet, but it'll do the job. Still smells a little smoky where the old one was.

We are back on the fields ready to play, and sometime durin' the second innin' things get a little wild. I don't know exactly when it happened because I'm steady focused on the issue at hand, which is the game.

In the top of the second innin', I find myself on first base from a bloop single. You probably know I'm ready to be on second base.

And they know I'm gonna steal. They know it! There ain't nothin' you can do but try and throw me out. Lonnie Gene was the ump again tonight, and he told me not to go in headfirst.

I said, "Lonnie Gene, you know there's one way to slide! Are you really tryin' to—" and I was off. I'll interrupt myself to steal a base. Mid-sentence I seen them pitch that ball, and I was on second base like a squirrel on a hot fry. Safe!

So, now I'm standin' on second base, and I see Mary Beth Tucker's horse hightailin' it across the outfield from the concession stand where she had him parked.

Then I start doin' some quick math. That horse is headin' toward Chet Dilroy's amateur archery course where they shootin' arrows at hay bales, and what do a horse eat? Bingo! So, that horse cleared the outfield fence—majestic, if you ask me—and landed on the other side.

Junior archers are scatterin' like minnows from a hand net. They was everywhere. And that horse just started munchin' on hay.

Well, now Mary Beth has abandoned her post at the concession stand. And she speed walkin' with one hand on her heart, like, *oh, Lord, Sarge. What are you doin'? I feed you!*

She's steady power walkin' across the field. She's callin' to that horse, "Sarge!" And that horse is just eatin'.

I'm standin' at second base, and we all turn, lookin' out past center field. Now Mary Beth is walkin' through center field, and her brother Russell Tucker hollers, "Get off the field."

He's right. At this point, there ain't no reason we can't be playin' again except that Mary Beth is speed walkin' it to the outfield wall. And I guess in her mind she would just take the same route as the horse, but she can't jump fences like no horse. She gets to that outfield wall, and I think folks are more interested in this part than when that horse cleared the wall.

Mary Beth reaches up on that wall like a toddler in a crib and then puts her hands back by her side. Now she's thinkin' about it. It's hittin' her that she's gonna have to climb. The fence is probably four and a half feet tall, but at some point, you gonna have to have both feet off the ground and on that fence if you really gonna climb over.

It's chain link with signs from different businesses—you know, advertisin'—and unless she's gonna just leap that fence, which she ain't, she's gonna have to drive the toe of one them tennis shoes into that chain link square. That's how you climb a fence. Super easy as a kid because your toes fit right in there, but as an adult that's a chore . . . and Mary Beth has wide feet.

She finally abandons that plan and walks around. At this point she's done speed walkin', so we are just waitin' on Mary Beth. She's got one hand on her side and the other hand thrown in the air. "Hold on! I almost got it."

I'm thinkin', *just leave the horse and go work the concession stand.* She finally makes it over there, grabbin' a fistful of hay and walkin' Sarge back over to the concession stand where she first had him parked. This time, when she gets there, she ties him up.

Them junior archers keep practicin', except one boy who was cryin'. He went home with his momma. And I turn around to see Rusty Tidwell at bat. Game's back on. Rusty doubles, so I'm off of second and headfirst into home plate before you know it—no throw to the plate. Safe.

Well, there are runners on first and second with two out in the bottom of the last innin', and we are ahead four to three. We got Myron Curtis at shortstop. They runnin' on contact, and they hit a single. Their runner on second takes off with his head down and runs right into Myron.

That fella falls down, but he's determined. He hops back up. But the impact with Myron shook him more than he thought, and he went right back down.

Russell Tucker throws the ball in from the outfield, and Myron tags that wobbly fella out. Game over.

I mean we woulda hoisted Myron high, but he's too heavy. Just ask that fella that ran into him. You could say what happened was a runaway horse, junior archery, Chet Dilroy's class in full sprint to safety, and Mary Beth Tucker speed walkin' . . . but I say it's a win. Do I care if Mary Beth Tucker brings her horse to the field next week? Neigh. See what I did there?[12]

So, where does that leave us? We lookin' at two-and-four now. That's respectable. You know they got them thirty/thirty clubs and forty/forty clubs in base-ball? Where they hit thirty homers and steal thirty bases?

Well, I'm shootin' for the five/twenty-five club this season. Five doubles and twenty-five stolen bases. That five doubles is ambitious I know, but you gotta set goals.

If Candy Dilroy can catch a full-growed crow, I should be able to hit five doubles and get the nursin' home to let me cut their grass. That's the way I see it.

---

12. *Editor's note: Neigh is a homophone for nay.*

8

JAWBREAKER

I guess we all know what it feels like to be down. And there's a number of reasons for that. Of course I ain't got time to list them all, but there's a few that come to mind.

Firstlys, you could have sprained your ankle. Or stirred up a beehive under the eave of a house. And C, you could be down because your softball team ain't winnin'.

Good news: Team Burger Shed is havin' some fun. It's just the way it is. Why? Because we won. That's it. That's sports, y'all. Take that to the bank, as they say. When you don't win, you start to look for fake wins.

"Well, we really executed with men on base to-night. And if we continue—"

No, you didn't! If you executed with men on base, you woulda pushed more fellas across home plate than the other team. You didn't *really* execute. You *kinda* executed.

"Well, our pitchin' is lookin' sharper."

It's adult league softball; there ain't no sharp pitchin'. You just lob that thing up there like a sponge in a bucket. What needs to be sharp is your fieldin'.

Catch that ball. Stop that ball. Throw that ball to first base and get some outs.

Before I get into that, I got an interview at the nursin' home! Not to be a resident, but to cut their grass. They want to talk next week. Things are lookin' up. Speakin' of lookin' up, Team Burger Shed is on the upswing.

We won not one but two games in a row. They are the only two games we won all season. We have lost four. So, you can imagine a couple weeks back when we was oh-and-four, how bleak it mighta looked.

They painted the new concession stand this week. It was just lumber color until this week. Now it's light blue.

Reason it's painted is because it's brand-new.

Reason it's brand-new is because Mary Beth Tucker burned the old one down tryin' to do s'mores by bringin' in a propane tank to a tiny wooden buildin' and lightin' marshmallows on fire.

You can say Mary Beth is real forward thinkin', tryin' to branch away from mustard dogs, sno-cones, and Skittles. But there's a reason that one sayin' is so famous: If it ain't broke, don't fix it.

Do s'mores at a campout. Do s'mores at home. Don't get all involved and messy at the softball fields. She's really askin' folks to cook their own food. Come on, Mary Beth.

The whole idea behind concession stand food is that you can get it quick and go back to watchin' the game you came there to watch. Or play the game you came there to play. Ain't nobody got time to cook their food—except little kids maybe. Then you got a whole 'nother problem tryin' to have a kid cook somethin' over an open fire.

So, the concession stand burned down; they cleared that spot and put a new little buildin' there. It's been there for a couple weeks now, but this was the first week since it got painted. It's lookin' good.

Maybe that was obvious to you, but it wadn't to Mary Beth. She actually said to the city council, "So, the next time we do s'mores . . ." And they cut her off at the meetin'. She had already said too much, and they told her in no uncertain terms that there will be no s'morin' around at the concession stand.

Well, if it ain't one thing, it's another, and tonight we was down a player before the game started. Do you even need to guess the name? Here's the deal: you might be thinkin' Brodie Childress since he's border-line reliable, but since we won two in a row he seems to wanna be there more. I'm tellin' ya, winnin' does that to folks.

If it ain't Brodie Childress then it's . . . you guessed it: Myron Curtis. Myron decides to have a jawbreaker before the game. Who cares, Tavin? Oh, Myron cares. And now our whole team does too.

If you gonna have a jawbreaker, before or after the game is a good call. Not durin' the game. So, I commend Myron for at least not doin' it durin' the game. You could choke on one of them so hard. The thing with Myron is that he's got one of them big ones. They are just shy of bein' as big as a tennis ball.

I mean if you manage to get that in your cheek you are droolin' like a baby. And that jawbreaker wedges your mouth open in a way where that drool just spills out. Then you pop that whole wet jawbreaker out and catch it in your hand, and it's bleedin' colors. Well, now you don't wanna hold that sloppy, wet, dense sphere of sweetness, so you pop it back in your mouth and repeat.

Giant jawbreakers are only a good idea. But they are an awful reality. I mean, think about it. Nobody has a picture of somebody eatin' a jawbreaker on the package of a jawbreaker. Nobody would buy that.

It looks like some form of punishment. You can't smile if you wanna because your mouth is wedged open and you are droolin' like a faucet. I guess you could smile with your eyes, but I digress because they ain't usin' people to sell jawbreakers. They usin' jawbreakers to sell jawbreakers.

The other thing you do with a jawbreaker, which leads me to Myron Curtis, is that you try and bite the jawbreaker to get it into more manageable pieces. I think breakin' a jawbreaker and breakin' a bowlin' ball is the same approach—drop it off somethin' really high and stand back.

But, course if you do that, you gonna lose the jawbreaker, so there's the dilemma. Why are jawbreakers still around?

Even the name ain't too pleasant. Oh, this breaks my jaw? Sign me up.

Them jawbreaker people have to be laughin' all the way to the bank. We don't need to show folks how to use it. We just gotta make it rock hard, big as a softball, and put speckled colors on it. And for some reason, adults and kids alike will be drawn to it. And somehow, they are right. Myron Curtis sure was into it tonight.

He is workin' on that jawbreaker maybe half an hour before the game. Droolin', gaggin', spittin' it out, catchin' it, repeat. And then he decides to bite it and try to break this thing down.

Well, one of them back teeth in his face broke off. Now, Myron ain't a baby. Sure, he had Mary Beth Tucker put a Band-Aid on a tiny scratch before, but that was more because he was datin' her and they flirtin' and all that. So, he ain't cryin' or nothin'. He actually tryin' to solve the problem. It ain't one of his strengths, but he's been around enough to know how.

So, he got part of his tooth in his hand, and he walks over to that light blue concession stand. He's already in his uniform, cleats, and sweat pants. He's ready for the game. And he asks Mary Beth Tucker for a couple of paper towels.

He drops that jawbreaker in one and sets it on the concession stand counter. He shoves his tooth shard in his front sweat pant pocket, and he jams that other paper towel in the back of his mouth to dry off the broke tooth part.

So, he's dryin' that thing and then asks Mary Beth for some super glue. Of course she has some because she uses it for warts and the sideview mirror on her Chevy Colorado that got clipped by a mule deer.

She hands that over to Myron, and he pulls the tooth out of his pocket with one hand and squirts super glue on that tooth—a generous amount. Real healthy glob of glue.

Now, I don't know if Mary Beth is thinkin' anything at all or if Myron sounds so convincin' that he has her mesmerized. Because normally if you see somebody super gluin' a broke part of their tooth and you know teeth belong in mouths then you think, *hey, maybe you shouldn't have super glue in your mouth . . . for a healthy number of reasons.*

Well, that don't happen. Nobody stops Myron, not even himself, and he jams that tooth up against the other half that is still in his head.

So, in his mouth at that moment was his hand, a paper towel, and half a tooth covered in super glue. You gettin' the picture?

He pulls his hand out and most of the paper towel,

but some of that towel got stuck back there on that tooth. I didn't go to school for super glue, but I think the chances are low of gettin' that paper towel back out of Myron's face.

And, as you well know, your tongue is in your mouth. And I don't know if Myron didn't think to move his tongue outta the way or if there just wasn't any place in his mouth for his tongue to hide, but he super glued his tongue to that broke tooth in the back of his head.

His eyes are wide. *Bink Bink.* He points at his mouth. And somehow that's enough for Mary Beth to know that his tongue is stuck back there.

So, she reaches under the counter for hydrogen peroxide. They got all kinda first aid stuff at the fields—probably just as flammable as a propane tank, but I ain't sure. They got a bee sting kit, wasper spray, dirt dobber detox, mosquito spray, all kinda Band-Aids, anti-venom, aspirin, you name it.

She tells Myron to gargle with the peroxide. That's what she told him. Said it would help his tongue come loose, but it didn't. Myron is tryin' to think but mostly startin' to panic.

He starts workin' that tongue and then reaches in his own mouth. He pulls hard. That tooth broke loose again, and it took off a bit of Myron's tongue. Just a little layer, but let's be honest—you know how your tongue gets when you go in too fast on a bowl of chicken noodle soup?

Well, this is way worse than that.

Myron gets a little wobbly at this point. I don't blame him. He's down. Can't play tonight. He ends up lyin' down on the tailgate of Rusty Tidwell's truck. A couple foul balls almost hit him, but he wadn't about to move.

That is a lotta mouth trauma, no doubt.

So, we have to play some softball without him, and the hardest hit I get tonight is off my shin in the third innin'. Them shin impacts will stay with you. I scored two times though. Russell Tucker and Rusty Tidwell are both makin' good contact, and they both hit behind me.

There are some sloppy plays in the field. I over-ran a grounder that ended up turnin' a single into a triple for the other team. I get queasy easily, and I think Myron's jawbreaker incident got in my head a little bit. Truth be told, anything on that list could be the culprit: broke tooth, super glue, garglin' with peroxide, or rippin' your tongue.

All of that is grounds for a goodly-sized dry heave.

Put it this way, we are a little bit better softball team this week than Myron Curtis is a dentist. Not much, but we played to a five-five tie, and that was it.

So, we played down one player and did not lose. Now, we are at two wins, four losses, and one tie. Not bad. Not bad at all.

I've got to get ready for the nursin' home interview. I'm wonderin' what kinda questions they are gonna ask, but I ain't wonderin' what flavor sno-cone to get.

I got a cherry sno-cone after the game. It wadn't free because we didn't win. That is one sweet treat that'll cool you off though.

Not like no jawbreaker, which will just get you worked up and possibly lead to injury.

We hope everybody is better for next week. Myron Curtis may have a quiet week ahead of him. I don't know how much talkin' he can do.

Myron was down, but I don't think we need to rub it in. That jawbreaker did enough.

ICE CREAM

Kevin Rickert and his brother run the grocery store in town. It's called Rickerts' Grocery Store. I don't reckon the store-namin' meetin' lasted too long when they decided on it. Don't matter nohow. Folks care about the price and the service.

Kevin had a rough day. That's what I'd call it.

There was a situation down at the grocery store with Delma Spencer. I ain't run the numbers, but I think somewhere in the eightieth percentile of all the chaos down at the grocery store is caused by Delma or one of her offspring.

So, today, I know Kevin was havin' a rough day. They had to cone off the ice cream aisle because somebody throwed up in a freezer. You heard me right. Not just in the aisle—although some ended up there. But like the freezer door is open where you pull out a gallon of ice cream or a box of Fudgsicles or that kinda thing.

You know the ice cream section. Maybe an ice cream sandwich, Drumstick, or Creamsicles. All kinda things like that, but they stay frozen behind them doors in the freezer section. You open the door to get the ice cream out that you want. Then you close them doors. That's how them doors work.

You are probably thinkin', *well, Tavin, I imagine it was one of Delma's kids that throwed up.* And nine times outta ten you'd be right.

But today, Kevin Rickert throwed up in his own freezer section. I know. It's gross and surprisin'. Turns out what happened was that he found a bunch of teeth in the freezer section. Like teeth from somebody's head.

I don't know what's goin' on in our town lately with all the teeth trauma, but I can't ignore the pattern. It's like a regular Hardy Boys or Sherlock Holmes mystery. Well, the throw up ain't no mystery. But why did Kevin lose it? I think he was restockin', reached down on a bottom shelf, and there was a heapin' handful of teeth kinda scattered down there. Some still had a little bit of gums on it. There was frozen blood on a few.

You can imagine how grossed out Kevin would be, and his reflex is to just throw up. So, he did. They cone off the aisle, and Kevin's hunch is to ask Delma. She's in the store already anyway.

He asks her if she knows anything about them teeth in the freezer section, and she looks back, no hesitation, and says, "Yeah, them's my babies' teeth."

Now, Delma's babies range from pretty newborn with no teeth to eight years old. And she got a step-son who is about twelve, I think.

So, Kevin asks her, "Whose teeth?"

She says, "Them's my kiddos'."

Kevin shakes his head and says, "Why in the world?"

"I just told them to toss their teeth in that freezer so the tooth fairy can get 'em."

"There ain't no tooth fairy in that freezer!" Kevin hollers.

"I ain't got no money to give them so I just figured maybe they'd get free ice cream."

That's gotta be the craziest thing Kevin ever heard. It's the craziest thing I ever heard. And I thought there's no way that Kevin would stand for this.

Now, he did say that she can't throw them baby teeth in the freezer section anymore. I'm sure he never thought that sentence would come out of his mouth. But it had to be said. If Delma didn't hear it, she'd keep doin' it.

So, Kevin hands her a baggy full of her own kids' teeth. Then, and this is where I'm tryin' to make sense of it all, Russell Tucker said he seen Kevin outside the store handin' Delma two gallons of ice cream!

Wait a minute! Did this really work out for Delma? I mean, she's bringin' home two gallons. Is she just gonna open the front door and say, "The tooth fairy came!"

Because them kids can't keep throwin' their teeth in there. Kevin's gotta know that throw up in the freezer section is bad for business.

The best I can tell, he just paid her off.

Like, "Here's some ice cream. Don't leave no teeth here ever again."

It was that or maybe he said don't ever come back in the store, so she had to wait outside while Kevin brought her the ice cream and she paid for it.

I doubt that though.

Don't matter nohow, I had a lawn to cut at the

nursin' home. That was basically the interview. I only have a push mower right now, but I borrow a ridin' mower or zero-turns for bigger jobs. My push mower could handle this job.

I'm about halfway through the job, and who do I see leavin' the nursin' home? It's Cricket in a cowboy hat, tank top, jean shorts, and sandals. I guess she's tryin' to keep the sun off her shoulders. I don't blame her.

I had some kinda feelin' sweep over me. It was like I had the chills, but I wasn't cold. She didn't see me, and I had to finish that job interview. Hopefully we'll connect soon.

At Team Burger Shed's game I seen Kevin Rickert walkin' to the concession stand. I guess he is tryin' to pawn off some of them all-natural, organic gummy bears down there because Bud already passed on 'em. Kevin can't barely give 'em away. But he's a business-man who's tryin' to minimize the losses as they say.

I see Kevin over there, and all I can think is that I sure hope he don't throw up by the concession stand. They just painted that thing. It's basically brand-new since that fire.

I don't guess there's a pile of bloody baby teeth over there though, so he's probably good.

TEAM BURGER SHED

Team Burger Shed is playin' pretty good ball. We ain't lost our last three games. We won two and tied one. So, we got momentum.

We got Myron Curtis back, who has been recoverin' from the self-dentistry he performed last week at the concession stand before the game. And I've been singin' the praises of Brodie Childress, who has been showin' up on time for our games.

Well, I'd guessed he was more interested because we was winnin', and turns out I was right. Why? Because we tied last week, and this week he shows up, but he wadn't dressed to play. He parked his sister-in-law's Dodge Neon in the parkin' lot just over the right field fence under the lights and was takin' pictures of it because she wants to sell it.

Like I've mentioned, just beyond center field is a pretty big grassy area—think of it like a fenced-in yard, and the reason they sectioned it off is so folks don't park in the grass.

A lot of these folks park in their own front yards, so it ain't gonna be nothin' to park on the grass at the city fields.

That grassy area is where Chet Dilroy trains them junior archers. That fenced area bleeds a little bit behind the left field fence, but there is some parkin' over on that side too.

I guess the easiest way to 'splain it is that on the left is parkin, in the middle is grass with a fence, and on the right is parkin', and Brodie Childress is on the right with that Dodge Neon.

The other team hits one home run tonight and one home run only. Not bad for us. The bad news for Brodie is that he is out there tryin' to get that car ready for sale when their homer sails over the outfield fence and lands right on the back windshield of the Dodge Neon.

It just shatters that thing. Brodie is hot, but he's the one who parked the car there. Everybody at the fields knows that you park over there at your own risk.

Myron Curtis yells at him from the outfield, "Slash that price!"

Brodie yells, "Shut your face, Myron!"

Myron shrugs and says, "You shoulda waited until after the game. You got a team over here that needs a center fielder."

We was playin' with two outfielders because Brodie was gone.

Third innin' I was up and hit a sharp single, straight down off home plate. It bounced so high! It's like a pop fly, but it ain't a pop fly because it already hit the ground. I was off to the races, just tearin' down that first base line. Pete Rose headfirst slide into the bag: safe!

They throwed it way over first base, and I got automatic second. I coulda kept runnin' and Pete-Rosed into second, but I thought, *I ain't gonna be like that. I ain't gonna showboat.*

I just walk over there. Then I got stranded. It was one-nothin' until the fourth innin'.

So, here we are in the fourth innin'. Mort Dwydell is up to bat. He hits a long single. And by a long single, I mean to the wall. It bounces, hits the wall, and rolls.

Mort ain't about to run. That ain't his strength. He'll make it to first on a blast like that, but I ain't never seen Mort leg out more than a single. He hits dingers. That's why we got him. Next, Myron takes a pitch off the shoulder.

So, now we got runners on first and second. Who is up to bat? I am up to bat. I'm a lefty. And they think I'm gonna pull it. They just ready for me to pull the ball.

But I don't pull the ball. I make contact, and that thing hits third base, inside the bag, and just pinballs into the infield—shortstop and third baseman are after it. They Keystone Coppin' it! Just convergin' on it at the same time. *Bink Bink!* What's about to go down, kinda thing.

Well, Mort is tryin' to get from second to third— his feet don't never leave the ground. I mean, Mort shuffles when he walks, but the shortstop was lyin' down reachin' for the ball, and Mort had to get around him somehow, so he jumps. Couldn't believe it.

Mort caught a little bit of air, and you know the ol' sayin' what goes up . . . well Mort came down, and it was not pretty. He did stick the landin'. Kinda wobbly, and when he hit the ground he hurt his back.

Anytime Mort has to move remotely fast, you kinda rootin' for no injury. Like a toddler takin' his first steps. But he is focused. He knows we've been on a tear. You can't make it to two wins, four losses, and one tie in adult softball leagues without a little blood, sweat, tears, and possible slipped discs in the back.

So, Mort is roundin' third like a three-legged pony. It ain't pretty, but he's movin' forward. The shortstop has finally crawled to the ball, but he ain't gettin' a throw off from his knees. Mort scores on what I'm callin' an infield single.

JT Whitlow and Myron Curtis went back-to-back in the seventh innin'. Myron's ball bounced up and hit the bumper of that Dodge Neon. Brodie yelled at Myron.

And Myron hollered back, "You had like five innin's to move that thing!"

We won five to three, so I'm guessin' Brodie is gonna want to play next week. We'll let him. We need another guy. He knows that. Plus it didn't really go well for him to skip a game. I don't know what he's gonna tell his sister in-law, but a Dodge Neon with a busted back window is gonna be a hard sell.

And me? I should find out tomorrow if I got that nursin' home job.

Quiet night at the concession stand, which is always a win. As far as I know Kevin Rickert is still stuck with them all-natural, organic gummy bears. Don't nobody want them things.

But, the way I see it, he'd rather be stuck with them than a bunch of Delma Spencer's kids' bloody, frozen teeth.

JALAPEÑO

You ever been to them warehouses and work-places where they have a sign posted that says how many days they've gone without acci-dents? Since the concession stand burned down at the city fields, I'm thinkin' that might help motivate Mary Beth Tucker to stay safe while she's workin' over there.

It's been weeks since the fire. I hope Mary Beth knows to stick to the basic snacks and not try to make s'mores and hot buttered dinner rolls that are softer than a baby angel's leg or nothin' like that.

As for Team Burger Shed, we've been feelin' pretty good. Like we have hit our stride. That bein' said, we did have a surprise this week at the fields.

Doreen Fundle is a nursin' home resident. I seen her son, Trot, down at the fields, and he told me he heard that I was the new lawnmowin' man down at the nursin' home. Really? Apparently that's what he heard when he was visitin' his momma today. Maybe that's as official as it's gonna get. I guess I'm hired!

Chlorine Phillips's son Gilbert was in town, and apparently they allowin' walk-ons now. He went to some junior college up in the Ozarks and was backup catcher there, so he has some 'sperience on the field and at the plate.

But the thing he's really known for is that he beat up an adult bull moose.[13] I mean, as the story goes, it wadn't just eye-to-eye, head-to-head, toe-to-toe kinda thing, but they went at it for upwards of three minutes.

Have you ever seen an adult bull moose? Buddy, they ain't tiny. I have a hard time imaginin' leanin' into one of them, like, *what you gonna do, moose?*

Anyhow, they went at it for a few minutes, and that bull moose end up turnin' or runnin'. Gilbert backed that thing down one way or another. I know that.

---

13. *Editor's note: We were unable to verify any such altercation and strongly recommend that you do not engage with any kind of moose.*

So, he's on the other team, and he steps into the batter's box. Mort Dwydell is our pitcher, and he is shakin' his head like he ain't gonna do this. He ain't gonna pitch to Gilbert.

Well, the ump do that little finger swirl in the air, you know, like, "Let's play ball. C'mon."

Mort shakes his head at the ump and hollers, "I ain't playin'. He's a pro, and he beat up an adult bull moose!"

Then Mort drops the ball right there on the pitcher's mound. He's really doin' this. So, I switch positions with him, and I get in there tryin' to find the strike zone.

Speakin' of strike zones, I consider Millie Ricks's house in a strike zone because I don't never know what I'm gonna get thrown at me. This past week I was ridin' by on my bike and she just hollered, "Pimento cheese and white bread!"

I heard what she said, but I did not know what to do about it. You know?

So, I automatically just said, "What did ya say?"

And she says it again, "Pimento cheese and white bread!"

Now, I didn't know if she was givin' me like the instructions for a recipe kinda thing or tellin' me what

I should have for lunch or what she is plannin' to eat later.

I just didn't know, so I say, "What about it, Millie?"

And she says, "That's the cure for everything."

Well, now I got a choice. I could just move on and wave and say, "Have a good day, Millie."

But I'm curious like a seagull near a Quarter Pounder. Kinda like one of them itches that just has to be scratched.

And I call out, "What can it cure, Millie?"

She said, "Oh, it can cure whoopin' cough, lockjaw, club feet, pneuomina,[14] diarrhea, canker sores, cleft pallette, chicken pox, strep throat, warts, procrastination, and dyslexia."[15]

I'm still tryin' to process that list when I realize she's starin' at me, waitin' for some kinda response. So, I knew I could go a couple different ways.

Firstlys, I could pose a question about any of them things Millie claims that pimento cheese and white bread cures. Like, *how does pimento cheese and white bread cure canker sores exactly, Millie?*

Because really even if she answered one, it would

---

14. *Editor's note: Pneumonia.*
15. *Editor's note: It cannot.*

have been the whole list I'd need to go down. Just wonderin' how she can even claim this stuff.

So, I don't even get into that with Millie. Not to mention she can't barely hear, so the more I yell at her the more she yells back at me.

I just try to back outta this strike zone, and I say, "Well, Millie, it's about lunchtime for me. I need to head on down to the Burger Shed."

And she hollers back, "Pimento cheese and white bread can cure that too!"

That was that. I was outta there and did not get no pimento cheese and white bread at the Burger Shed. Firstlys, because I don't want any today, and B, Bud don't serve it anyway, but I did get a bacon double cheeseburger. That worked out well.

I might try that pimento cheese soon. I have had a little trouble with procrastination.

Meanwhile, back at the fields I can't find the strike zone. The ball is all over the place, and don't think my mind didn't wander back to the two-hitter I threw here recently.

So, I admit I'm a little 'timidated by Gilbert standin' in the batter's box waggin' that bat above his head. I'm doin' my best to focus, but I get distracted. There's a commotion in the stands, and runnin' under the bleachers is Jalapeño. That's what Cheryl Grubbs named her new dog.

Cheryl and her husband, Shane, live on three acres. She decided to take that dog into town with her here recently to run errands. Now, I ain't no dog whisperer or nothin' like that, but I'm pretty sure that dog would rather be out on that three acres instead of in the back of a Chevy Cobalt runnin' errands in town.

The first stop Cheryl made with Jalapeño was Maggie's Flowers—it's the flower shop in town—and that dog went in there and peed all over the floor.

Maggie handed Cheryl a mop and said, "Clean that up."

So, while Cheryl is over there cleanin' that up, ol' Jalapeño eats a bouquet of flowers—chrysanthemums, marigolds, and poinsettias. I don't know all my flowers, but you take one of these kinda flowers and one of them kinda flowers and put it together and it makes a bouquet.

Well, that dog munched the top off them flowers to where they was just the stems. And he ate a burger Maggie left sittin' on the counter too. Maggie couldn't get Cheryl and Jalapeño outta there fast enough.

Next, Cheryl went to the bank, and that dog

followed her in there and knocked over a water cooler. Flooded the entrance to the bank—water all on that carpet . . . *squish squash, squish squash.*

Dorothy Adkins, an older gal in town, walked into the bank, and she's got on them orthopedic shoes. They got soaked. And them don't look 'spensive, but they are.

Cheryl says, "I just needed to get the dog out. That dog needed to get out."

I told her, "Cheryl, that dog was on three acres. It *was* out!"

Get that Chevy Cobalt home, Cheryl.

Apparently, she still thinks that doggie needs to see the town. So, she's got it runnin' the softball fields, and I see her hoofin' it after Jalapeño.

Unless Jalapeño decides to slow down or stop, Cheryl ain't got a chance. About that time JT Whitlow hollers at me. "Tavin, you gotta pitch that thing!"

I zoned out there for a minute, and I think my team was thinkin' I was about to chicken out like Mort did. But that ain't it. I know the damage Jalapeño can do, and I was just watchin' to see how bad it might get in the bleachers.

So, I toss one down the middle, and Gilbert is ready. He turns on that ball so hard and sends a screamin' line drive down the third base line, where it finds Rusty Tidwell's shin.

It sounds like somebody bounced a cue ball on a driveway. You know if you get popped in the shin by a horseshoe or a softball, it'll take you out for the day, maybe longer.

Rusty is the most athletic member of Team Burger Shed. He's a beast, but there ain't nothin' you can do when Chlorine Phillips's son Gilbert lines a screamer off your shin. All you can do is what Rusty did, which is go down like a newborn fawn on a frozen pond.

So, we moved JT Whitlow over to third, but honestly, we was out of it the rest of the game. They got in our head bringin' a ringer into the game like attaway. So, we just tried to finish the game the best we could. And the best we could do tonight was seven to two.

Myron Curtis, of all people, decides to give a pep talk after the game. He's sayin' we gotta man up, and we can't just walk away when we are scared. Mort has his head hung down.

I don't know if Mort didn't pitch because he was really that scared or if he thought the ump would say, once Mort took his stand, "No, Gilbert, you can't stay.

You ain't on that team or even signed up in this league." Whatever his reason was, it sure was a bad look now.

I start thinkin' about runnin' into Cricket at the nursin' home, which takes my mind off the loss.

'Bout the time Myron is really lettin' us all have it about bein' a man, his girlfriend Mary Beth hollers that her momma is waitin' for them down at Bickham's All You Can Eat Catfish Buffet and they need to get. So they got.

Then, a ten-year-old fella, winded-like, holds Jalapeño's leash tryin' to return that dog to Cheryl. I tell her she needs to get that lad a sno-cone and leave that dog on them three acres. If she's not careful, that doggy is gonna run and keep goin'. Ol' Jalapeño may be too hot to hold on to. *Bink Bink.*

So, if you are keepin' track, after tonight we are three, five, and one. Was it fair, them bringin' in a ringer like that? Nope.

Do we make excuses though? Kinda actually. But I'm over it.

I know these things have a way of workin' themselves out. I just need to stay healthy and hydrated this week and show up ready to play. Maybe I can't beat up no adult bull moose, but I can put a hurtin' on a Dr Pepper. So, that's the plan.

TEAM BURGER SHED

The concession stand ain't had no injuries in two weeks, but Team Burger Shed has to start our count over. Rusty's gonna be nursin' that shin this week.

KITTY CAT

Millie Ricks brought a "therapy cat" into the veterinary today. Millie's somewhere in her eighties or nineties, and she can't hear too well or see too well, but she got the energy of a young rat terrier. And it happens in spurts.

I started at the nursin' home early and cut the grass. Apparently I was too early for Cricket. She was not there.

Then, I took my mower to the veterinary where I got hired to cut their grass—that's where they have like doctors and nurses for animals. And they see 'em all—dogs, cats, wood finches, horses, cows, and bob-cats. They even had a peacock and a Shetland pony.

Our town is known for ponies, so there's been quite a few through there.

Mary Beth Tucker went to school for horses, and that's her main job. One time she told me that peacocks and Shetland ponies are mean, and it can be temptin' not to help them.

Well, today, I'm mowin' the back lawn there, and folks start pourin' out like it's a fire drill. I'm mowin' the lawn—push mower, mind you—and it's loud. So, I cut off the mower when I see folks movin' like that.

Mary Beth got her thumb pointin' back over her shoulder, "Millie Ricks!"

Usually when somebody says Millie's name, they ain't runnin' in fear. I mean, she can surprise ya, like when she filled a Super Soaker with sweet tea and sprayed me when I was tryin' to mow her lawn. She sure thought that was funny, but it was not. Bein' sticky is bad enough, and then when bees and dragonflies wanna make you their party spot, it gets worse. So fast.

"What's wrong, Mary Beth?"

Mary Beth is huffin' and puffin', kinda doublin' over. "It's not a cat."

I'm thinkin', *okay. What in the world is Mary Beth talkin' about?* I know the whole story now because I'm on the other side of it, but I didn't at the time. All I see is Mary Beth run out and say it ain't a cat. What ain't a cat?

About that time Millie Ricks walks out the back of the veterinary steady holdin' a skunk. Apparently, they are easier to catch than you might think.

She's lookin' around, confused at the commotion, and I don't even know if she's aware that she's the one causin' it.

"My cat needs a bath!" she hollers.

I take a step toward her, and I look at that skunk. Buddy, I know a lotta folks are scared of skunks. It's kinda the same reaction when folks see snakes. It ain't about what they *are* doin'. It's about what they *can* do.

But that skunk was as scared as we were. I'm pretty sure by the look on that skunk's face that it ain't never been cradled like a baby before, and it was not sure what to do next.

I didn't even know if that thing had already skunked Millie. She wouldn't know, because she can't smell, and maybe the skunk knew it would be a wasted effort. It's like skunk's kryptonite is somebody who can't smell, and that's Millie.

I don't really know, but I knew that Millie had to let that skunk go. It wadn't her cat no matter what she said. And it didn't need a bath. It's a skunk.

So, I say, "Millie, what ya got there?"

She said, "A little kitty cat."

"Can you let it go?"

"Why?"

"Because you don't own a sku—a cat that color."

"What color is it?" She looks down at that skunk curiously, and I think I heard that skunk say, "Please, Tavin," like it was rootin' for me. I think Millie's grip loosened. She's answerin' my questions with a little doubt in her mind.

Now it's like a hostage negotiation.

"Millie, go ahead and put that cat on the ground."

"Oh, it needs a bath."

I told her cats give themselves a bath.

She said, "They ain't got thumbs."

"I understand that, Millie, but it'll lick itself, and you ain't gotta worry about it."

"I wanna dry its hair."

Then I said, "Well, go get your hair dryer."

She said, "Oh, good idea!"

And she was off. She let that skunk down. It bolted, and whatever lesson it needed to learn, I could tell it learned it by the look on its face.

Nobody got skunked, but it sure scared folks because it wadn't gonna bolt back in the buildin', and everybody else was standin' back there with me on the lawn. It headed our way, and folks scattered. The only other times I seen Mary Beth Tucker move that quick was when she hoofed it outta the burnin' concession stand with the cash box and when she got tossed off of Myron's moped. He's still learnin' to handle that thing.

So, this all happens before our softball game. Lots of chatter about that skunk and how I talked Millie Ricks outta givin' it a bath. As a businessman, I get in these situations and gotta know how to deal with folks.

In last week's game, Chlorine Philips's son, Gilbert, who played backup catcher one year at a junior college in the Ozarks and beat up an adult bull moose, played for the other team. They whooped us seven to two. We got word this week that they are doin' playoffs this season, but we three-five-and-one, and that ain't playoff material . . . yet.

You never know what can happen in a few games, and we basically trendin' the right direction. We really are. Last week was a mess for a few reasons, but mostly Gilbert. I know that I said I ain't gonna make excuses, but I will say Gilbert was a big reason that we got so messed up.

He don't even live in town. He's gone now. So, he basically showed up, played one game—the game they played Team Burger Shed—and he's gone. That's fine. We ain't quitters. And I'm just gonna leave that right there. Like half a sandwich you find on a park bench. Don't pick it up.

Well, now we are playin' for our lives so to speak. We don't know if we can make them playoffs, but we sure can't go if we only win three games all season. So, we gotta keep winnin'. We are tryin'.

Let me ask you this: Who had a good night at the plate? Who walked twice tonight, got hit by a pitch, and had a soft single? Then, in the seventh innin', hit a dribbler in the infield? Tavin Dillard. That's me.

The dribbler in the seventh seemed like a routine play. But, if you've spent much time around adult league softball, there is rarely a routine play.

Kurt Pickney picks up that dribbler. He's playin' third base. He also plays third for the high school team. He's got an arm like a rocket, and he fires that thing to first base. And it just sails. Up, up, up! It flies all the way out to the second parkin' lot, all the way under a tan Buick with white doors.

They can't find it, and whoever hit that ball gets to take second base. So, I did.

Mort Dwydell bats behind me tonight. He turns quick on the first pitch, and before you know it, we are both standin' at home base. Home run Mort. He hits dingers.

After that, it's one thing after another, we are a scorin' machine, steady smellin' them playoffs. We score seventeen, and they score twelve. Everything seems to be clickin' on all cylinders right now. I mean, everything but our pitchin'. Thankfully we were playin' a team with the same problem. Their problem is a little bit worse than ours.

That puts our record at four wins, five losses, and a tie, and a step closer to the playoffs. So, all I really know is that we won this week. We won so hard.

Have I mentioned that winnin' teams get free sno-cones at the concession stand? Team Burger Shed made our way over there after the game, but the only flavor left was coconut.

You may have already figured this out, but our concession stand ain't winnin' any awards. It just ain't. I told Mary Beth Tucker that I'd pass on the free sno-cone this time.

I just biked to the Burger Shed and got a Cherry Dr Pepper. I think the owner of that Buick drove off with the softball. You ain't 'posed to do that. It ain't a souvenir.

But if you can't find it, you can't find it.

TEAM BURGER SHED

And now we feel like we in the hunt! I highly recommend softball league hunts. Huntin' skunks? No, thanks. I really don't know if Millie ever got her hair dryer, but there is a skunk out there somewhere with his little head on a swivel.

DONUTS

Let's say you wake up hungry for a donut. So, you get dressed and head to the donut store for an apple frittler.[16] You are walkin' into the store, and there ain't much of a line. So, you figure you either beat the rush or missed the rush.

But since you ain't sure if you early or late, you don't really know what you are gonna find inside that display case. It could be full, or you could be lookin' at three cake donuts and a lemon-filled powdered and that's it.

You have your heart set on the apple frittler. You

---

16. *Editor's note: You probably got this one, but in case you didn't . . . apple fritter.*

scan them donut pans. The frittler pan is empty. There ain't one left. Now you have a choice to make. Are you gonna go without that frittler that was the size of a pillow? I mean you had big plans for it: take it back to the trailer, pop it on a paper plate with some butter on top, nine seconds in the microwave, and then eat it with a fork like a sit-down meal. That ain't gonna happen now. What do you do?

But then they bring out a chocolate Long John and standard glazed twists. And you remember that good plans can interrupt your day too. Reason how come I say this is because we got some good news for Team Burger Shed today. More on that shortly.

One time, Ricky Don Pierson—he's a volunteer firefighter—had to help get Candy Dilroy off the roof of a house. It wadn't her house. You already know she lives in the same trailer park as me. She catches crows but apparently can't get off the roof of a house. Somehow she can get up there though.

She thought she saw a personal-sized pizza on the roof. You know, one of them little ones that will feed one person. So, she got on the roof, and it turned out it was most of a frittler. Then she couldn't get down.

That's when her folks realized she probably needed

glasses, so I guess that's the silver linin'. And she got to keep that frittler, which personally I thought was gross. A crow coulda licked that thing or done who-knows-what to it.

Woulda been poetic justice for the crow, I reckon.

The point is that you don't wanna get sidetracked. I highly doubt that Candy was walkin' through neighborhoods lookin' for personal pizzas on the roofs. No, somethin' caught her eye, and off she went.

Who cares, Tavin? Why are you tellin' stories about empty frittler pans and Candy Dilroy on a roof?

Sometimes things happen and they work out better than we thought. And sometimes we can get sidetracked by things we think are good, but they make things worse. Clear as mud?

Well, let me tell you what we learned about Team Burger Shed today.

You already know we've won four games, lost five, and tied one. But, hold onto your sweat breeches because I got some breakin' news.

I'm as excited as a squirrel in a bag of hot fries. Here's the deal. Two weeks ago we lost to a team that brought in a ringer from out of town. I know I said I wadn't gonna bring it up no more and I wadn't, but there's news about that game. So, how do I not talk about the new news without bringin' up the old news? That's just science. Probably.[17]

So, Chlorine Phillips's son, Gilbert, who had played backup catcher one year at a junior college in the Ozarks and has beat up an adult bull moose, played on this other team. He ain't never been on the team before, but he was visitin' from out of town and just hopped on there for a game.

They whooped our team. Gilbert almost single-handily whooped us. Mort Dwydell refused to pitch because he said it wadn't fair. They got in our heads bringin' Gilbert in like that. And anyhow, we lost seven to two.

So, when I tell you that we have lost five games, I actually have to correct that. We have only lost four now because Gilbert disqualified them for that game by playin'.

Their team lost a win, and we lost a loss. I mean, if there's anything you wanna be a loser at, it's losses. Now we are four-four-and-one. That ain't a bad place to be.

But, where does that leave us? Well, here's the deal. I can't hardly stand it.

The way the math work out on this season is that because we only lost them four games, just by takin'

---

17. *Editor's note: It is not.*

away that loss, mathematically it puts Team Burger Shed in the playoffs. So, before the game even starts, we are already in the playoffs.

And, even better news, I said hi to Cricket! I seen her droppin' off produce at the Burger Shed when I was ridin' my bike into the parkin' lot. I hollered, "Hey, Cricket!"

She didn't answer. Then I seen her climb into her truck and take out some headphones she had in her ears. I guess she listens to music while she makes deliveries. But I did say hey. That's a start.

This playoff news leads to a whole new situation. Which is, how are we gonna play this game comin' up in a few minutes? Because what happens is that you can change your mindset.

None of us thought about that before the game. We was just excited. Nobody thought, "Hey, what if they got that math wrong and we actually have to win tonight?" None of that crossed our minds.

In fact, what crossed Myron Curtis's mind was that he should get nachos at the concession stand with extra jalapeños *before* the game. Mary Beth Tucker brought nachos tonight to the concession stand.

It's never enough just to have some hot dogs, sno-cones, and Skittles. Nope, she's tryin' new stuff out like some sort of fancy chef. She ain't. She's at the softball fields' concession stand.

So, she brought in a crockpot of cheese and was ladlin' that out into paper bowls. I have no idea why she didn't see a problem with servin' Myron them jalapeño nachos before the game, but apparently that was not on her radar.

So, we all kinda giddy leadin' up to game time.

Speakin' of leadin', guess who is battin' lead off? Bingo! First pitch I go up there swingin' and foul one hard off my leg. It stung. I kinda walked a little lap and circled back to home plate.

The next pitch I'm locked in, and it shows when I make soft contact to shallow center field. They got their second baseman out there. He picks that thing up and tries to throw me out from there. I overran the bag, and he hit me in the back with the ball, and that kinda stung too.

We are two pitches into the game, and I'm on first base. I've already had a ball fouled off my leg, and now I been hit in the back. But I'm on base, and when I'm on base, I steal the next one. I'm a base-stealin' machine. But my leg was throbbin', so I decided to stay put on the first pitch.

Mort Dwydell connected on what woulda been

a triple for most folks, but he just made it to first. I made it home though. So, we was off to the races, you might say.

And then Myron Curtis, for bein' able to put away so much food, has got them tender guts. The nachos hit him pretty hard between the second and third innin's, and he shuffled over to that park bathroom in a hurry, steady hopin' he don't put on a show before he gets there.

And Myron's the kinda guy that if he ain't feelin' well, he wants the whole world to know. And them park bathrooms echo. Hearin' it was pretty gross, but it mighta worked in our favor. We need all the help we could get because we were down a player from the third to the fifth innin'.

So, we just had two outfielders in the third in-nin', and then what we did was pull the catcher. Cody Briggs went to center field. We played the fourth and fifth innin's without a catcher.

We scored a couple runs. Then they score a few. It was three-two in the third innin'. But Rusty Tidwell, per usual, was locked in. He ended up goin' four for five with two homers.

We got Myron back in the bottom of the fifth. He just looked a little fatigued, and he told us in the dugout, "I can't run, y'all. I'll lose my bowels."

"Myron, why in the world are you havin' jalapeño nachos, extra jalapeños, before our last regular season game? And I know Mary Beth gave you extra, so it wadn't even the standard amount you 'posed to get."

He did still play, but he was like quarter speed, which was like a hair better than havin' a foldin' chair on the team. I mean, we was rootin' to win, but we was also rootin' for Myron not to mess his breeches tryin' to get to first base.

Well, most of us. Rusty Tidwell can have a sick sense of humor sometimes.

Let me just tell you this though—by the end of the game it was nine to seven, Team Burger Shed. Now, we five, four, and one, and we headin' to the playoffs.

Rusty Tidwell brought some expired Kit Kats that his sister-in-law got from her work, so we was all feelin' pretty good. And even after Myron's nacho bout he reached in that bag Rusty brought and got himself a couple of them Kit Kats.

He said they was for the ride home. Well, he was on his moped, and I could just imagine him tryin' to tear into one of them while he's steerin'. He's liable to start wobblin' and then lay that moped down.

I told him, "Just wait 'til you get home, Myron.

It ain't that big of rush. Them Kit Kats are already expired."

And I told Mary Beth Tucker not to bring no jalapeños next week to the concession stand. We can't take no chances.

I may take another chance this week and say hi to Cricket for real, if I have the time.

So, that's that. I don't know who we are playin' first in the playoffs, but I do know that we are in the playoffs. And that's a real good thing. Basically like havin' a pan full of apple frittlers.

ONE INNIN'

This week was the first week of playoffs for Team Burger Shed. There was a time when we was chest-naked, no uniforms, and no team name. We have come a long way.

And why do I care about the first round of playoffs? Because we made it! We weren't sure about the schedule. They said we have to make it down to the fields where they post the playoff schedule on the side of the concession stand. They also post it on the inter webs.[18]

Our games all season have been on Thursday nights. Well, not this week. We go down there

---

18. Editor's note: The internet.

Thursday night, and that schedule that's posted on the concession stand says we don't play 'til Friday. It was kinda relaxin' just bein' down there on a game night but still having one night before we need to play.

I'm down there shootin' the breeze with folks. Cheryl Grubbs is there. She actually got stuck in a bike rack down at Rickerts' Grocery Store here in the last year or so. I'm not sayin' that's what she's known for, but I am sayin' that happened.

The thing about it is, nobody can figure out how she got stuck. Not the fire department or the police department. I mean, they can only go off what Cheryl said, and she ain't sayin' much.

I don't blame her. If you're a full-grown adult and you get stuck in a bike rack in front of the grocery store, that's embarrassin'. Not to mention, Cheryl ain't got a bike. So, it ain't like she was over there lockin' up her bike and got all tangled like attaway.

You ever seen them curly metal games you get from Gatlinburg or somewhere, where you try to unlink them things, but the more you try, the more frustratin' it gets? That's how I imagine it was for Cheryl in that bike rack.

They had to cut the thing. You can still kinda attach a bike to it, but it ain't the same. I imagine Kevin

Rickert sent her the bill.

Anyhow, Cheryl is down here along with all kinda folks from town, and it's kinda like a carnival atmosphere. I mean, there ain't a cotton candy machine and rides, but if Mary Beth Tucker heard me say that, she'd sure try to get cotton candy in that concession stand. Seems like she has tried everything else.

I've said it before and I will say it again. Stick to the basics, Mary Beth. Sno-cones, hot dogs, and Skittles. It ain't rocket scientist.[19]

But there is some business we did have to handle at the fields Thursday. Like, what time do we play Friday? Who are we gonna play? Well, we find all that out, and then it's on to the big show.

This is what you really wanna know. How did our first playoff game go? We was anticipatin' this game. I ain't gonna speak for everybody, but I sure was anticipatin'. It was different goin' to bed on Thursday night thinkin' about the game on Friday. Some butterflies and all of that.

We was set to play Bickham's All You Can Eat Catfish Buffet. They big boys. And you probably wanna know how we matched up. Well, on paper, not great.

---

19. *Editor's note: You don't really need me to clarify this, do you?*

They only lost two games all season. So, we was better at losin', but we knew we just had to play our game. Folks say that all the time. Do you know what that means? Me neither.

I guess it means, *hey, you know how to play. Go do that.* So, that's what we did.

We go three up and three down in the top of the first. Then, it's the bottom of the first, and we are on the field—defense. Bickham's is up to bat.

JT Whitlow is playin' second base for us, and they hit a grounder right at him. It was almost too good. Like, he probably would have fielded it better if he had to range a little bit one way or the other. But that thing just eats him up.

He drops the glove down, but that ball don't even hit his glove. It musta hit a pebble or somethin'. We got a gravelly infield. They ain't like big rocks but them tiny ones. And they will cause some trouble.

Them first two weeks of the season when we didn't have no uniforms yet and I was stealin' bases headfirst, chest-naked, I felt every pebble out there.

So, that ball bounces right before JT's glove, hit his forearm, and just kept speedin' up his arm, onto his neck, and hits him right under the chin.

You ever been hit in the face and still had to do

somethin'? Usually all your friends are around, so you're tryin' to keep it together, but you ain't sure where to go or what noise is appropriate to make.

Well, JT still has to find that ball and at least act like he is gonna finish out that play. So, he keeps the ball in front of him—thanks to his chin—and then he just picks it up, and they had a runner on first.

And it wadn't just JT. The next batter lines a screamer to Rusty Tidwell, Mr. Reliable over there at third base. It's in and out of his glove. The runner on first waits to see if Rusty is gonna catch it. Once he don't, that fella tears out toward second, and Rusty could get him easy, but JT ain't on the bag, so Rusty just fires it to first, over Mort Dwydell's head. And that's that.

Two batters into the game, and there ain't no outs, with runners on first and second. Their third batter up grounds it to Mort at first. Mort shuffles the ball to nobody coverin' first. Cody Briggs is pitchin', and he is 'posed to cover it, but he don't. Then Mort jumps on the softball like a grenade, and he rolls and taps the bag with his foot.

We ain't got instant replay in the adult softball league, but quite a few folks are sayin' Mort got that fella out, but he was called safe, and the bases are loaded.

The next one is a no doubter. Fly ball to center field. Brodie Childress caught it, but that runner on third tagged up. We are down one to nothing with one out.

Next fella hits a single, and they move station to station. Bases loaded again. And then they fire off two doubles in a row that scores three more runs, and by the end of the first innin' we are losin' four-nothing.

For all that anticipatin', we sure are off to a rough start. Such a rough start.

Then somethin' happens to me. I have this thought in my head: That's just one innin'. And I go back to the dugout and see the fellas, and they're dejected. It was tough to be in a four-to-nothing hole against the big boys from Bickham's All You Can Eat Catfish Buffet.

I think some of the most memorable speeches in history ain't long. You know Winston Churchill gave like a graduation address not too long before he died and made it up to the podium and just said to them graduates, "Never, never give up."[20] That was it. And I bet they didn't forget it. That's an easy speech to remember.

---

20. Editor's note: The National Churchill Museum notes this speech as taking place at Harrow School in October of 1941 (https://www. nationalchurchillmuseum.org/never-give-in-never-never-never.html).

So, I ain't sayin' I'm a Winston in the dugout, but in my mind I'm thinkin', *that was just one innin'*.

So, I holler, "One innin'!" Everybody turns because I holler like I'm mad, but I ain't mad, just determined and resolved, you might say.

Like I made a New Year's resolution right then and there, except there ain't no new year; it's just the first innin' of our first, and maybe only, playoff game.

Everybody is lookin' at me. So, I say it again, "One innin'!"

Myron Curtis shrugs like he don't get it. And that's when I think maybe this speech is makin' more sense in my head.

I say it again. "It's just one innin'! We only played one innin'!" Heads start to nod. I point at the whole team. "Are y'all done?"

Fellas are shakin' they heads no.

Then I go one at a time. I mean, I look every teammate in the eye one at a time and point right at their chest and say "One innin'" to Myron Curtis.

"One innin'" to Mort Dwydell.

"One innin'" to Rance Farnhart.

"One innin'" to Cody Briggs.

"One innin'" to Russell Tucker.

"One innin'" to JT Whitlow.

And I say "One innin'" to Rusty Tidwell. I woulda said it to Brodie Childress too, but I think he went to the bathroom.

One innin'.

Then all of a sudden Rusty shouts it back. And Rusty don't typically shout. Rusty is good at everything he does, so his actions speak louder than words. But right now his words are speakin' louder than words.

And somethin' about Rusty gettin' worked up gets everybody worked up. Our whole dugout is shoutin', "One innin'." And for a second I wonder if that didn't make no sense to all the fans and the other team. You know, like if it sounded weird just to be shoutin' "One innin'."

But then I realize, this ain't for them. It's for Team Burger Shed. We get it. And that's all that matters. So, here we go.

And while all this is goin' on, I see Cricket holdin' a sno-cone headin' to that truck of hers in the parkin' lot. It might be her daddy's truck. It's the one she uses for them deliveries. I'm wonderin' if she heard that speech I just gave. Well, I can't be thinkin' about that right now.

I'm up first in the second innin'. I don't waste time. I swing away and made a little contact, soft single. Got on first base easy like that. And I don't stay on first that long. I would steal a base when my team ain't even battin' if I could. I am a thief on them base paths.

But Myron Curtis is battin' right behind me, and, truth be told, we all a little pumped up, so nobody's waitin'. Myron swings and lines one to center field on a bounce. Runners on first and second.

JT Whitlow is battin'. He sees a ball outside but decides to take a swing, and it pops straight up. Now, I don't know what me and Myron are thinkin', but we run. And JT is runnin'.

And that ball shoots so high in the air, like a bottle rocket with a real strong fuse. It flies so high up in the air where you ain't sure if it's gonna come back down or not, but you know it's gotta because of gravity. And it do.

But JT just keeps runnin'. He said later he couldn't control that ball, but he could control his legs, and he kept runnin'. JT is yellin' at Myron in front of him, "Go, go, go, go, go!"

We are bookin' it! And the fella on Bickham's drops the ball. You can either run it out or be a spectator. JT Whitlow ran it out, and we got two runs. That's how the second innin' closes out for us. The score is four to two, but now we have the momentum.

Then there is the fourth innin'. Rusty Tidwell makes soft contact, which is rare for him. He usually strikes that thing with some power. He bloops it into right field for a single. He's on first, and Mort Dwydell is up.

You know by now that Mort only has very long singles or home runs. Once he makes it to first and it ain't a home-run trot, he's done. From that point on, he's base to base.

So, he's up with Rusty Tidwell on first, and Mort makes serious contact. Serious. That thing went way out into the parkin' lot.

Chet Dilroy's nephew, Tony Wayne, was out there. He had a four-wheeler accident recently where he got a rib outta place. He reaches out to get that ball, and he has a rib go out again. Tony Wayne is laid out in that parkin' lot. He's arm is stretched out tryin' to reach that softball, and he can't quite reach it.

The Cromwell boy, maybe six years old, runs up and snatches that souvenir. A medic hustles out there and says Tony Wayne's gonna be okay. And the league collects them softballs, so that six-year-old has to give it back, but he gets to trade it for a sno-cone. That's how it works.

That two-run shot by Mort brings us even at four-four. Looky there, won't ya?

So, let me take you to the last innin'. I drop in one of my patented soft singles. I'm on first. We still tied four-four. I'm hungry for a steal. That pitcher releases that ball, and I'm off to the races. Headfirst, Pete Rose into second. No throw. Safe.

The pitch was a strike on Myron Curtis. Now, they pitchin' again to Myron, and I'm off. Headfirst, Pete Rose, this time they throw—late. And now I'm standin' on third with no outs.

Well, just when Myron is about to get pitch number three, it's like a swarm of dragonflies or cicadas or somethin' comes through, and Myron takes a swing at them bugs with his bat while a ball is headin' toward the plate.

He hits it!

It's a dribbler down the first base line. Myron's got the whole bench hollerin' at him to get down that line to first. And he's off. So, there's Myron lumberin' down the first base line. And as he starts lumberin' attaway. I start headin' home!

The first baseman picks up that ball, and he can't get it past Myron. Myron carry some girth, and he's in the middle of the base path where he belong—just bearin' down on first base.

That first baseman's throw lands right in Myron's gut. And his tummy kinda catch it like a mitt would, and it falls to the ground. I slide across home plate. Safe!

Bickham's has the last at bat, and I guess they are feelin' in the last innin' how we was feelin' in the first. Just down and out. Dejected. Well, they don't snap out of it.

They swing for the fences three times and pop out three times. And that, my friends, means Team Burger Shed is goin' to the second round of the playoffs.

JT Whitlow says his chin hurts a little less after the win. I get it. Winnin' handles all kinda problems. So do free sno-cones. There's some fireworks in the trailer park tonight.

But we ain't done. Team Burger Shed still has work to do.

TIRES

It might as well be the openin' day of turkey season or even Christmas mornin'. Team Burger Shed is deep into playoff softball right now. Are we excited? You better believe it.

A few weeks ago, lookin' at our numbers you would not 'spect that we would be in the playoffs. And ain't that just like life? You 'member David and Goliath? David was a little feller, and he decided he didn't really care for this giant Goliath and all his mockery. Well, nobody else was standin' up to Goliath, and the king told David he could take a crack at him.

He gives David some armor and stuff men wear in battle. But all that gear just weighed him down too much. He got five stones and a sling and went to battle.

And that young fella said he got God on his side. He only needed one stone to take down Goliath, and buddy, that turned the tide. All the Philistines who was so brave behind that giant turned tail and ran. 'Member that?[21]

Well, I ain't sayin' God is on Team Burger Shed's side, but I am sayin' didn't nobody 'spect this. But here we are, we've done won our first game in the playoffs, and we're about to play game two.

I ride my bike to the softball fields. It's like a silver BMX bike, but it ain't that brand. But it kinda look like a BMX. You know like that's what the frame or body style is. It's what some folks might call a knock-off. I just call it my bike.

I'm ridin' it to the fields for some playoff softball. I wear my uniform and hat, so I ain't gotta hold them, but I do have my glove. I'm a lefty. I figure you know that by now. And there's a couple of ways I carry the glove. One is that I just hold it in one hand. Now, I don't mean wearin' it like attaway, like you'd wear it at the field. I mean, just holdin' it and basically ridin'

---

21. *Editor's note: This is a surprisingly faithful retelling of the story of David and Goliath.*

my bike with one hand.

Another way is to sit on the glove. Just put it on my bike seat, but the thing about that is that if I stand up, then it's gone. So, if I do it that way, I really gotta be focused, and honestly when I'm on my way to a game—especially a playoff game—I don't need that kinda extra thought takin' up space.

The other way is a bungee cord, and I can strap that thing to the handlebars or the seat or the frame. I can do any of that. And that's probably the best option, so I can have both hands on the handlebars in case I need to ramp a curb, jump a mud puddle, or even do a frame stand if I'm really feelin' it on the way to the ball fields.

Well, today I'm just holdin' the glove. And I am a block and a half from the trailer park when I hit a speed wobble. And I ain't goin' that fast. I quickly discover that I got a flat tire. I say speed wobble, and that makes it sound like I was breakin' records, but it's like a speed wobble where the handlebars shake and they jerk back and forth real quick and you don't know if you gonna stay up or lay that thing down.

I look down and see my front tire is flat. And it really coulda been anything. A shard of glass, a nail, or barbed wire. My own brother coulda stuck a screwdriver in it.

But that ain't my concern right now. Because it's the front tire—and I can pop a wheelie so hard—I could just do that. But poppin' a good wheelie takes some serious mental effort, and I'm already thinkin' about this playoff game. So, I just hop off the bike and walk it to the fields.

I just decide, you know what, I'm gonna figure this out later. So, I'm holdin' my glove and walkin' my bike to the fields. And that's how the evenin' begins.

We are playin' Brunwell Tires. Lonnie Brunwell is on the team. His daddy owns Brunwell Tires, and he come in there with his 2007 1500 Dodge Ram. It's big. It's loud. He got a CB in that thing with a speaker on top.

And he pulls into the parkin' lot behind home plate and says, "I ain't parkin' in the outfield lot, because I'm gonna be hittin' dingers out there all night."

So, he parks back there and is doing a showboatin' kinda thing. He's right. He starts hittin' dingers to right field all night long. What he wadn't countin' on was Mort Dwydell and Rusty Tidwell hittin' foul balls onto his Dodge Ram all night.

Now, we ain't tryin' to do this. Believe me, they are tryin' to hit it front ways and just don't get a hold of a few. They fly back and don't shatter the windshield, but you can eat a bowl of Cap'n Crunch outta the hood of his truck now. And we ain't necessarily proud of that, but that's just how it's happenin'.

Brunwell Tires is out hittin' dingers though. For real. They are up six to one, quick. It got away from us pretty fast in this one. Now, the third innin' rolls around, and I get up there to the plate, and I hit a double. Now, I don't hit it too hard or too far, but Brunwell Tires is a whole team of hitters, and they ain't really runners. So, if you hit it on the ground through the infield, you liable to get two. And that's what happened, y'all. I'm leggin' out a double.

Nothin' came from that double, but in the fifth innin', Rusty Tidwell steps up with two on, and he hits a three-run shot over the right field fence. He gets us back in it a little bit. And somebody's car got hit.

Wadn't Lonnie Brunwell's because he made a point not to park in the outfield tonight. And it hit that car in the lot on a bounce. I mean, it's just the risk you take. Myself, I ain't got a car or truck, so there's pros and cons to that.

I mean I did get a flat tire on the way to the game, but that ain't just a bike thing. You could get a flat on a car too. And you got more chances to get a flat with a car because you got more tires on them. Another good thing about my bike is that it don't get hit by foul balls. It's a smaller target. I park it behind the dugout and lean it against there, so it don't see the foul balls like attaway.

But Rusty finds that parkin' lot out there in the fifth innin'. Now it's a ball game.

And you wanna know who was hittin' it hard all night? I mean, this fella ain't never had a night at the plate like this: Myron Curtis. That's right. The fella who got all this started back at the Burger Shed with Mort Dwydell. The guy who not only forgot to bring our uniforms to the first two games but never ordered 'em in the first place!

And here we are in round two of the playoffs. We got our Team Burger Shed uniforms on—lookin' like a team, playin' like a team—and Myron Curtis is makin' some serious noise.

I seen Mary Beth Tucker crane her neck outta the concession stand at one point when he was battin' because she heard the contact he made. It was impressive. I ain't gonna lie.

Only thing is, every ball he hit tonight was right to somebody. And that's the way that Brunwell Tires likes to play. If they ain't gotta move, all the better.

TIRES

We played hard. They played hard. And by the end of the game, Brunwell Tires pushed across eight runs and we pushed across five. So, quick math'll tell ya that they won and they movin' on to the championship game.

They say if you gettin' exercise you winnin'. You know, like, you might not win the game, but you still stayin' healthy. I mean, I guess there is some consolation in that, but losin' stinks, best I can tell.

We played almost as many games as we could this season. Just one game shy of the championship, and I do think that's a good thing. The whole team was a little down after the loss, but Mary Beth Tucker made sugar cookies. The truth is, sugar is sugar, and them cookies were good though.

The fellas start to clear out of the dugout. Nobody is sayin' too much.

I'm kinda leanin' up against the chainlink fence there outside the back of the dugout, and I hear some gal holler, "Hey!"

I hear her holler, but I figure she ain't talkin' to me, so I just kept workin' on that sugar cookie. Then I hear, "Hey, Tavin!" And I'm the only Tavin on our team—only Tavin in our town that I know of—so I look up, and who do I see? That's right. It's Cricket.

So, I try to pull it together and say, "What are you up to?"

And she said, "I'm workin' for my daddy this summer deliverin' produce in town. You heard of the Burger Shed?"

I look down at my Burger Shed uniform and then back up to Cricket and said, "I sure do know about the Burger Shed."

She said, "Maybe me and you can get some lunch there and catch up some time."

Now, some folks might say I got a way with words, but there are times where I just ain't sure what to say. I look at Cricket and say, "I like burgers."

And then she replies, "Great!" and off she goes.

You ever heard when one door closes, another opens? I don't know what's gonna happen with Cricket, but I sure am glad that this happened at the last game of the season and not the first.

I know what Myron Curtis was like back when he first started datin' Mary Beth Tucker—head in the clouds. He's still kinda that way, but he can manage it better now. He ain't blowin' kisses roundin' first and disappearin' to snack on a hot buttered dinner roll that is softer than a baby angel's leg.

So, here I am. I walk my bike down to the Burger

TIRES

Shed after the game, and while I was pushin' it down the street I was thinkin' about Brunwell Tires. Maybe they could fix my bike tire for a discount.

You know? They gotta be feelin' good after their win. Can't hurt to ask.

TEAM PARTY

It's hard to believe this season came and went. I look back over my shoulder, and I remember a black nanner way back when I first heard about the season. It was a midnight, turn-out-the-lights, full-black nanner.[22] But I made it through all that.

And to think Myron Curtis was the fella in charge when it all started. Say what you want, but he got it started. I'm glad he did. We went from no name, no uniforms, to a playoff team called Team Burger Shed.

As far as I'm concerned, you're on the team too. Now, you ain't invited to the team party, but that's only because I ain't got your address.

---

22. *Editor's note: Back to basics. A very black banana.*

Team Burger Shed

Where do you think we had the team party? Well, if you are havin' trouble guessin', I got one word for you: read our uniforms. That's right. We partied at Bud's Burger Shed.

I arrive a little bit early. It's about suppertime, late afternoon, and there's plenty of folks there. Bud ain't about to shut down the Burger Shed for a team party, so we just had to figure that out ourselves. We didn't get no trophy for third place overall, but we did get a certificate, and we had it framed. I'll tell you right now, Bud cracked a smile when he seen that.

"What's this?" he asked, smilin'.

"That's the third place certificate. We figured you could hang it on your wall," I told him.

He went from reluctant sponsor to smilin' business owner. That made me feel better about askin' him to sponsor us all them weeks ago. You want to change a situation? Win.

I'm tellin' ya, winnin' helps quite a few things out. And losin' just exposes what you need to work on. Like, don't eat jalapeños before a game. Come on, Myron.

JT Whitlow shows up wearin' his glove. He's sayin' we should do a team photo. Rusty Tidwell shows up straight from work, hungry, and he didn't have his uniform, just his work shirt. Well, remember what I said about winnin'?

Bud let Rusty and Mort Dwydell borrow shirts for a team photo. But wait, there's more. Bud brought out all kinda burgers, curly fries, and drinks. I'm tryin' to collect money, and Bud stops me.

"This is on me, fellas. Good season," he says, and he smiles again.

That's a pretty big deal.

"What in the world, Bud? I can't imagine what you woulda done if we actually won the championship," I told him as I hand money back to the team.

"Why don't you win it next season and find out? I'd probably just do this again though."

Makes sense to me. Free food seems to be like the ultimate team party win. Cody Briggs put away a couple burgers. Brodie Childress was late, of course, but he ended up with some food. And then we could finally take the team picture. We got Russell a gift card to the tractor supply store since he basically coached our team.

I wish I could say Myron's head is out of the clouds, but it ain't. Mary Beth showed up to Bud's with two baskets of hot buttered dinner rolls that was softer than a baby angel's leg. Finally, the team could try them.

Rance Farnhart told us that he'd give free haircuts to anybody on the team this week. We just need to make it out to the patio at the Bait and Tackle Shop. Winnin' sure feels good. We didn't take the championship, but we started one place and ended up somewhere better.

Ain't that the idea? I'd like to think we even learned from the losses. I know one thing. We went to battle, and we had a good time doin' that together. Pretty much everybody smiled for the team photo. We had to take a few because we forgot to ask Bud to be in the photo the first couple. And then Mort's eyes kept closin'.

Mort had a milkshake tonight too. So, from what I know about Milktrate Refugee,[23] he's headed for some tummy trouble. He may want to give his wife and kids a heads-up so she can pack a bag for her momma's. He says they can't stay in the house when he gets a hold of too much dairy.

I'm takin' Mort's word for it.

I don't know about next season yet. I do know we got somethin' to build on if we decide to field a team again. Once you get a taste of winnin'—and free snocones—it's hard to walk away.

---

23. *Editor's note: Still lactose intolerance.*

And if you have learned anything from this season, you know I don't walk anywhere. I am runnin' and divin' headfirst into the next thing. So, I got my eye on Cannonball Season at the city pool, some bike rampin', and this new gal who is back in town.

Will I win? I don't know. But the only way I know is if I get on the field and play. That's what happened this season. And that's how Team Burger Shed came to be.

Now, if you'll excuse me, I told Bud I'd sweep the floor after the fellas leave. And he said he'd gladly pay me in curly fries. That's what I call a win-win.

ABOUT TAVIN DILLARD

Tavin Dillard is a mowin', edgin', grass cuttin' legend. He began building an online audience in 2006 and has welcomed many awesome fans into Chancellor Park and his neck of the woods since then. He has a weekly podcast, performs live comedy shows, and he wrote a book. You are holdin' it now. Find out more at SweetTeaFilms.com or search Tavin Dillard on Instagram, YouTube, or TikTok.

ABOUT JOEL BERRY

Joel Berry is a husband, father, writer, actor, and comedian. He believes people are very important creations of God and we are all looking for connection with God and each other. The right stories connect us and bring refreshment. These are the stories he strives to tell.

WANT MORE TAVIN DILLARD IN YOUR LIFE?

LIKE ISSAWAY
LIKE ATTAWAY

TAVINDILLARD.COM

TEXT TAVIN: 501-322-6249

Visit SweetTeaFilms.com to sign up for Tavin's mailing list. You can also buy personal greetings, shirts, stickers, and much more. Including Bacon. Plus, you'll find Tavin's upcoming live show dates, his podcast, and more funny videos!

GET YOUR TEAM BURGER SHED GEAR TODAY!

VISIT SweetTeaFilms.com

MORE FROM BEST MEDICINE BOOKS!

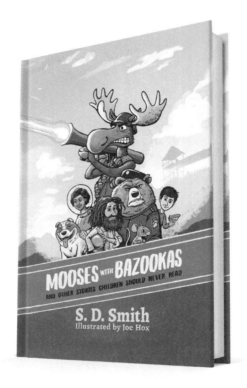